Hope for the Future

An Advent Journey for Bereaved Parents

By Laura Diehl

Hope for the Future

An Advent Journey for Bereaved Parents

When Tragedy Strikes: Rebuilding Your Life with Hope and Healing After the Death of Your Child, Copyright 2106, Laura Diehl
Published by Morgan James Publishing (New York)

Come Grieve Through Our Eyes: How to Give Comfort and Support to Grieving Parents, Copyright 2015, Laura Diehl

My Grief Journey: Coloring Book and Journal for Bereaved Parents, Copyright 2016, Laura Diehl

ISBN: 1981291016

ISBN-13: 978-1981291014

Table of contents

Instructions	1
The Word "Pareavor"	3
Introduction	7
Week One - Hope	9
Week Two - Peace	37
Week Three - Joy	65
Week Four - Love	93
Christmas Day	117
Going Deeper	121
About the Author	123
Other books by Laura Diehl	124
Visit us Online	129
Laura Diehl, Speaker	131
Laura Diehl, Coach	133

Instructions

When Do I Start?

Advent begins at a different time each year. It can start as early as November 27, or as late as December 3. You can either Google it for the year we are in, or you can easily figure it out, since it always starts on the 4th Sunday before Christmas. (Which means the fourth week is usually completed during the week of Christmas.)

What Will I Need?

You don't need to have your own advent wreath, but you may find that lighting the advent candles each evening adds to the depth of the experience. Advent wreaths can be purchased at various stores (including online) or you can do an internet search to get lots of ideas on how you can put one together yourself.

If you were to research what color of candles to use for the advent wreath, you would find they are usually purple and pink. However, I decided to use colors that made the most sense to me personally, based on the word it represents in this unique view of advent (which will be explained in the readings each week).

Green - Hope
Blue - Peace
Yellow - Joy
Red - Love

White (center candle - can be a pillar candle) - Christmas Day

Many stores have the various colors of candles needed. My recommendation is Hobby Lobby, if you have one in your area, as they have all of the colors in various sizes.

How Do I Know When to Light the Candles and Which One(s) To Light?

In each reading, you will be instructed which candles to light and when.

How to Join the Author Live Each Week

Starting on the first night of advent, and the following Sunday nights through the advent season, I plan to be live on our Grieving Parents Sharing Hope Facebook page (www.facebook.com/gpshope) and share the reading and lighting of the candles with those who want to join me. (As of the time this book was published, it will be at 8:30PM Central time. I will inform and remind everyone each week on the GPS Hope Facebook page, so you will be able to confirm the time there.)

Still Have Questions?

Please feel free to contact me, Laura Diehl, directly at laura@gpshope.org.

The Word "Pareavor"

Pareavor? What does that mean?

I am so glad you asked.

After our daughter, Becca, died, I knew there was no word that could even come close to describing my pain. At the same time, I wondered why there is not a word for those of us who are living here after the death or our child. Someone who has lost their parents is an orphan. My son-in-law became a widower, and of course, a woman whose husband has died is called a widow.

This started to really bother me.

I think it is important to have a word that validates the fact that parents who have lost a child through death have a weight that is extremely heavy...heavier than most will experience in this life. **Not as a label to give us permission to wallow in our deep sorrow, but one that draws us together to be able to strengthen and encourage each other within our life-long club membership that none of us wanted.**

At this point, let me quote from my book, *Come Grieve Through Our Eyes.*

> As a parent who has experienced this horrific event, I found myself trying to think of a word to describe what I felt, and the only thing that came to me is *death*—the pain of my own death. A part of us dies along with our child.

...I have thought and prayed long and hard on this. One day I sat down and listed all the words possible for parents, grief, bereaved, children, etc. to see what I could put together as a word for a grieving or bereaved parent.

That is how I made the word: PAREAVOR. A pareavor is a parent who has lost a child through death. How did I come up with this?

"Pa" comes from the word parent: a person who is a father or mother; a person who has a child (Merriam-Webster)

"Reave" comes from the word bereave. The meaning of the actual word "reave" (which the word bereave comes from) is: to plunder or rob, to deprive one of, to seize, to carry or tear away (Merriam-Webster).

"Or": indicating a person who does something (Wiktionary)

This sounds like a pretty good description of what happens when our child dies, no matter the age of the child. So, **a "pareavor" is a parent who has been deprived of their child who was seized and torn away from them through death.**

I have met several bereaved parents who love the word, but were not sure how to pronounce it, so let me share that with you as well.

"pa" is pronounced like the u in p<u>u</u>ff

"reav" is pronounced like it sounds in the word be**<u>reave</u>**

"or" sound is the typical "er" sound like moth**<u>er</u>**

pu reav' er = pareavor

Feel free to steal the word and use it, if it resonates with you.

And if you ever see me, please ask about my pareavor/hope bracelet. I would be happy to show it to you and give you one to wear as well, as a way to connect with others who are in this same club. It is also a visible reminder we often need that we are not alone, and there is always hope.

Introduction

When we face the death of our child, it can feel impossible to believe God is for us, or with us. So many unanswered questions, many that start with "Why."

The end-of-the-year holiday season can amplify everything, especially the questions and the pain.

Even as I am writing this, I have had to stop and cry, with sobs that I have not had in quite some time. I can barely see through the tears to continue.

But no matter how much pain I am in, somehow, I know that God is the only one who can truly help me.

A few days ago, right before Thanksgiving, I was before the Lord and the words, "Emmanuel, God with us," hit my spirit with almost an explosion. I cried out, telling the Lord that I want Him to be with me every day of this next month. I want to feel Him; I want to know His peace in a very tangible way.

I suddenly had a picture of our advent wreath. As our children grew up, we had many years where we did the advent wreath to help refocus us, from the commercialism and the frazzled busyness of the season, to Jesus.

The thought came to me to have my own advent time with the Lord each night, using the wreath and the candles, based on the symbolism of the hope, love, joy and peace we have through Jesus, who is Emmanuel, God with us; to have a time where I specifically focus on who He is within my pain of the loss of my daughter.

I decided not to do it alone, but to include anyone who has the same desire and cry in their heart. The first year, I went live on Facebook each night during the advent season, lighting a candle and sharing something about the word it represented.

The following year, I decided to change things up a bit and only do a live candle lighting on the four advent Sundays, and turn my "script" into a book, which is what you now have in your possession. (You can find out how to join me and others live on the mentioned advent Sundays on the instructions page.)

There are so many other things you could be doing with your evenings. I do not take it lightly that you would consider using your valuable time to read and meditate on what God has spoken to me about what Christmas means to us now as pareavors.

May you be deeply blessed and find a measure of healing as you focus on making this Christmas season one of reflecting on our Savior in the midst of your painful loss. I sincerely pray that in the next few weeks, the Holy Spirit will remind us all that no matter how suffocating the darkness, there *is* hope for our future, because He truly is Emmanuel, God with us.

Week One - HOPE

Day 1 - Sunday

So, what exactly is "advent?" The word itself means a season of waiting; more specifically, it is waiting for Jesus to come. Many people will do something to acknowledge advent during the end of the year as a season of waiting for Christmas, when we celebrate the birth of our Savior.

As pareavors, we are also waiting for Jesus:

- Waiting for Him to take away our intense, suffocating pain
- Waiting for Him to explain Himself, to tell us why He allowed such a horrible thing in our lives
- Waiting for Him to reunite us with our children

And that brings me to the word we will be talking about this first week. We can wait with HOPE.

1 Thessalonians 4:13 says, "Brothers and sisters, we do not want you to be uninformed about those who sleep in death, so that you do not grieve like the rest of mankind, who have no hope" (NIV).

The Word of God doesn't tell us not to grieve. God doesn't want us to grieve without hope.

The way we use hope isn't the way the Bible uses the word hope. We use it like, "I hope it won't rain tomorrow." We use the word hope more like a wish we want to come true. "I hope I get a new computer for Christmas."

God uses hope in a different way. When He is involved, it is a seed we plant that leads to faith. Hebrews chapter 11 tells us that faith is the evidence or assurance of things we hope for. This kind of hope is like a woman who has been given an engagement ring. She has a secure hope that she will be getting married. (Faith is more like when she is getting dressed to walk down the aisle – the evidence or assurance of what is hoped for, of things not yet seen.)

We can grieve with hope, a secure belief, that God has a plan, and that plan is to reunite us with our children, never to be separated again.

This world isn't our home. We are just passing through. And for some reason, my daughter, and your daughter or son, passed through sooner than we did.

Everything in us screams, "that isn't right!" God knows that, which is why we can grieve with the hope that someday it will be *made* right when we join our child, and the suffering we faced in this sinful, crappy world will be forever behind us.

For those who might have a fear that their child wasn't saved, allow me to quote from my book *When Tragedy Strikes.*

> *God's love for your child supersedes your love for him or her. Each one of us is created with His desire to have an intimate relationship with us, not just here on earth, but for all of eternity. I believe God is big enough to have made every opportunity possible for your child to accept Him before leaving this earth. This could easily have happened during a time you know nothing about (including crying out to Him at the moment of death). So give that fear to God, trusting that He took care of it. Not having the information you want to have doesn't mean it did not happen at some point in their lives.*

I hope that gives peace to many of you, as we start this four-week journey together.

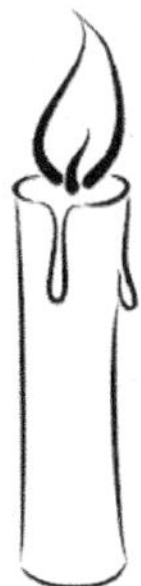

(LIGHT THE GREEN CANDLE)

Yellow often represents an emotion like hope, but I have chosen green for this advent time.

Why?

Because green is the color of life, new growth and restoration. That sounds like hope to me!

For those of us who live in places like Wisconsin, where all four seasons are seen clearly, it is an understatement to say we are looking forward to seeing green life appear after a long winter!

And guess what? No matter how bad our "cabin fever" gets, it *always* happens! Spring always follows winter. New buds come out and everything starts turning green with new life.

Life always follows death, including our own death that we experienced on the inside of us when our child left this earth.

It is important to realize that God's specialty is bringing life from death.

I have noticed how often something I have read many times previously in the Bible now has a totally new meaning since Becca died. I want to end today's time by sharing one of those scriptures with you. It is Job 14: 7 "There is hope for a tree that has been cut down; it *can* come back to life and sprout" (GNT).

I felt like I had been cut down when Becca died, with no life in me. But I eventually discovered that wasn't true for me, and it isn't true for you, either. Not only is there life, but there is potential for growth to flourish once again. But there will always be the stump where life was cut off, and where life began again.

Prayer: Father, thank you that you tell us it is okay to grieve. And thank you for showing us why we can have a secure hope within that grief. Amen.

Day 2 - Monday

This first week of advent, we are thinking about hope. Last night I talked about how God tells us it is okay to grieve, but He doesn't want us to grieve without hope.

Tonight, I want to talk about how our perspective affects our hope.

> *I can either focus on my personal loss that my child is permanently absent from this earth, or I can focus on the fact that my child is absent from this earth but present with the Lord, and even though the pain is intense, I will meet up with my child again in our eternal home, never to be separated again. It may not seem like it, but our perspective is a choice we make. I strongly recommend you choose the second perspective, saving yourself lots of torment.*
>
> *To get through this to be able to live again, we cannot lean on our own understanding. In all our ways we have to acknowledge the truth that God is always good, whether we agree with His decisions or not. In order to change my feelings, I have to change my perspective.* (Taken from *When Tragedy Strikes*)

I remember the exact moment my perspective changed, giving me hope for the first time that I really could get to a place of light and life again after Becca's death.

I was at the cemetery. I stood at Becca's grave, looking around at all the tombstones, many of which I had read (especially noticing the ages of some who were much younger than Becca). I suddenly realized that each one of those tombstones represented a family who had faced deep grief, and were somehow able to move forward with that person no longer with them. If they could do it, I knew it was possible, and that somehow, I could do it, too.

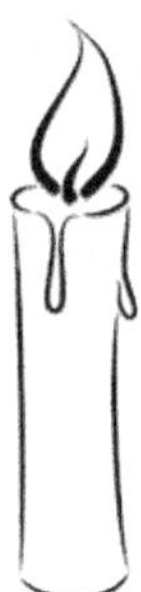

(LIGHT THE GREEN CANDLE)

As I shared in the introduction, normally the advent candles are pink and purple. But I decided to choose my own colors for the candles in looking at advent through the eyes of our grief. For hope I chose green because green is the color of renewal and new life.

Tonight I want us to think about a scripture that is familiar to most of us.

Psalm 23: says–"The Lord *Adonai* is my shepherd; I have everything I need.He has me lie down in grassy pastures, he leads me by quiet water, and he restores my inner person" (CJB).

God restores. He has everything we need. When we hear that, we might say, "I *need* my child back!" But we know that isn't going to happen.

What many of us need is to stop asking God why, and start asking Him how. "God, *how* are you going to get me through this? *How* are you going to be my shepherd and give me everything I need to live again, and not just live, but live a fulfilling life? *How* are you going to restore my inner person and heal these deep, deep wounds left by my child being amputated from me?"

You see, a person who has an amputation learns how to adapt; how to live with that part of them missing. I know this first hand, because Becca, our daughter who left this earth, had her leg amputated when she was only three years old. It was horrible when it first happened, but she learned how to live with one leg missing, and lived a very full life for the next twenty-six years, even though she was constantly faced with the reminder of her loss; both the limitations and how it made her different from those around her.

Losing our child is like having a very part of us cut off.

I can testify along with hundreds and thousands of other pareavors that it can be done. You *can* have hope, that God is everything you need, *especially* after the death of your child. He *can*, and wants to restore your soul.

We will never be the same person as before, but we can learn how to live a life with meaning and purpose once again.

Prayer: God, we need to change our perspective. Some of us need help even wanting to change it. Let us see through Your eyes, showing us what we need to see.

Day 3 - Tuesday

I read somewhere that waiting, trusting, and hoping are like three strands of a rope. Trust is the middle strand, with hope and waiting being the two strands wrapping around it.

This is a good description of how I have gotten to the place I have, with the grace of God. I have chosen to trust God in the midst of the deep pain and darkness, while I wait and hope on Him to somehow help me get to a place of living a fulfilled life once again.

And talking about waiting brings us right back to advent.

Advent is a time of waiting; waiting for the coming or arrival of something. This is the season when advent is waiting for the arrival of Christmas. For most, it is a time of joyful anticipation, mixed with frazzled busyness.

But for many of us who have faced the death of our child, it is a time of waiting for the season to just... be...over. There are so many painful reminders of who we are missing, and painful reminders of what will never be.

We are also waiting to be reunited with our child, and that can't seem to come soon enough. I remember in that first year after Becca died, telling God to just kill me, so I could be done here. Even though I had four other children, I just couldn't get past the pain of having Becca gone, to be able to enjoy and love the ones who were still here.

Most of us are not suicidal. We just don't want to live any more. I believe God knew from the very beginning of time that we would struggle with feeling so hopeless in our grief, and He did something about it.

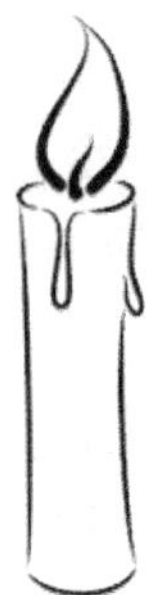

(LIGHT THE GREEN CANDLE)

1 Peter 1:3-5 tells us that we have an inheritance reserved in heaven; a living hope through the resurrection of Christ from the dead.

Even though the Christmas season is all about Jesus entering the world of the humans He created and becoming one of us, the purpose of His birth was to die, so that we could have life. Not just life after we leave this world, but abundant life here on this earth (John 10:10). And believe it or not, He still wants to make good on that gift, that promise, in *your* life, after the death of your child.

God tells us that He is near to the broken hearted (Psalm 34:18). I don't think there is anyone more brokenhearted than those of us who have lost a child.

But no matter how broken you are today, tomorrow always promises new hope.

Allow God to plant His seed of hope right in the middle of your pain, and watch it sprout into life.

Romans 15:13 has become one of my absolute favorite verses since Becca died. Please see this as a special gift during this advent season for yourself. "Now may the God of hope fill you with all joy and peace in believing, that you may abound in hope by the power of the Holy Spirit" (NKJV).

Right now, let's speak God's hope into our hopelessness together.

Prayer: God, You are the giver of hope. We take this time to come into agreement with Paul, that as the God of hope, You will fill us with joy and peace in our believing, so that we will abound in hope by the power of the Holy Spirit. Amen.

Day 4 - Wednesday

Is something not true, just because you don't believe it? During the winter, while everything is covered in snow, if I decide to believe the grass isn't green anymore and it is going to come up blue, does that make it true?

People talk about truth being relative - that I can decide what is true for me, and you can decide what is true for you. But where do we draw the line if we each get to decide what our own personal truth is? If I decide *my* truth is that there is nothing wrong with taking something that belongs to you if I want it bad enough, is it okay for me to act on *my* view of truth without consequences? Obviously not. Life doesn't work that way.

Something (or someone) has to be the standard for what is true, and what is not. And that standard cannot be set by people. The world's standard of truth (or what is right or wrong) is always changing. That line is always moving. A great example of that is when television first came out, actors who were playing the part of a married couple were in separate twin beds if there was a bedroom scene. Those lines kept changing, until now it isn't thought much of at all when an unmarried couple are ripping clothes off of each other down to nothing while being filmed for public viewing.

There is only one standard that is *always* the same; only one place truth comes from, and it is God and His Word, and that is whether I chose to believe that truth or not.

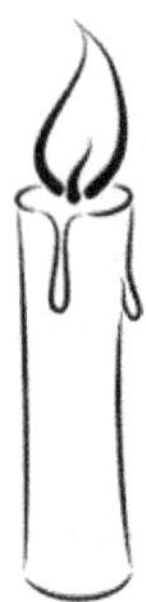

(LIGHT THE GREEN CANDLE)

Mary was engaged to Joseph. In Jewish culture, this was a marriage contract, but the ceremony to physically consummate their marriage had not yet taken place.

When the angel Gabriel appeared to Mary, the first thing he said was that she was favored by God and that He was with her. He then proceeded to tell her God's plan.

From Mary's viewpoint, God was putting her in a place where she would be stoned for becoming pregnant (especially when it wasn't her fiancé's baby). That doesn't sound like she was favored by God to me! Those of us who know the whole story from beginning to end can say, "Yes, God was right. She was highly favored." But within that moment, the end couldn't be seen by Mary. That didn't mean God wasn't speaking the truth. It just meant the truth seemed to conflict with what was happening because Mary couldn't see what God was seeing.

After asking some valid questions, her response was absolutely amazing. "I am a servant of the Lord's. Let it be to me according to His word (or His will)." Wow!

Have you ever said something like that to God? Maybe the words were more like, "Jesus, be Lord of my life." Or maybe, "God, everything I have is Yours." But now we are finding out that maybe we didn't really mean those words... we didn't know it meant Jesus would allow our child to be taken from us, did we?

And now we might be struggling with that truth. We want to change it, or at least change the results of the truth that He is Lord of our lives. But we have to remember that God can see the full picture. He can see what we cannot see, and He knows what we do not know, just like He did with Mary.

The truth is, He is near to the broken hearted. The truth is, Jesus is the Alpha and Omega, the beginning and the end and He has the final Word in our lives. The truth is that He came as a baby, born to bring hope and light and life to our messed-up world.

So, make the choice to believe the truth, even if you feel like God really messed up big time. Emotions are not what the truth is based on. Remember, Jesus *is* truth Believe the truth that there is hope to live again after the death of your child. Believe that if we surrender to the process, we place ourselves on the path that takes us to that place of hope.

Just because we can't believe it in our place of darkness, doesn't mean it isn't true. The truth sets us free. If nothing else, have hope in that fact.

Prayer: God, we want to believe. Help our unbelief. Set us free to believe the truth; that we can have hope because You have a plan we cannot see, and that we can trust that plan, even in our place of darkness and confusion. Amen.

Day 5 - Thursday

We are in a time of advent, a time of waiting for the arrival or coming of something or someone. As I said before, many of us who have lost a child are just waiting for this Christmas season to be over.

We just want to receive our promise of heaven, to be reunited with our child.

There are so many people in the Bible who had to wait for what God promised them. Noah and his family did a lot of waiting. When the rain started, they had to wait 40 days for it to stop. They were actually on the ark a total of three hundred seventy-eight days, by the time the water receded enough for them to get off the ark and back onto dry land.

When Moses led the Israelites out of slavery, they were left wandering in the wilderness for forty years before being led into the land they were promised. As a matter of fact, it was the children of those who were led out of slavery who received that promise.

When the Messiah was first promised to come and set mankind free from the bondages of sin and death, it was several thousand years later before the waiting was over and the promise was fulfilled.

And when Jesus left this earth, his disciples had to wait for the promise of the Holy Spirit to come live inside of them.

Waiting is part of life. But it is easy to lose hope when we have to wait. And many of us are still in a place of total darkness after the death of our child.

If you can't see any light, if you don't feel any hope, it's okay. We have all been there, as bereaved parents. Just keep waiting, y, one minute, one breath at a time. Wait for that hope ıo come to you. It may come as a dim flicker, or it may come as a bright light, but it *will* come!

And while you wait, make sure you stay connected to other pareavors who can be an anchor of hope for you, until your own hope breaks through.

When we have no hope, we have no desire to live.

We know the enemy is out to steal from us and kill us. If he can't do it physically, he will do it emotionally. When our child dies, we have the biggest red target on us for the enemy to do exactly that. He steals our hope, leaving us wanting to die to go be with our child. Even if we have other children, a wonderful marriage and had a life full of purpose and passion before our child's death, it all comes crashing down and we are left in a world of darkness and hopelessness.

However, the death of our child did not blindside God like it might have done to us. This means we do not have to stay a slave, chained to our prison of darkness with no hope. Jesus came to break every chain that could ever try to keep us bound. He will carry us through this valley of death, back into a place of abounding hope. (Taken from *My Grief Journey*).

(LIGHT THE GREEN CANDLE)

Christmas is about light. Hope brings light. The light is always there, even if we are in a darkness too dark to see it. The sun is always shining, even if the clouds are covering it, or it is nighttime and the sun is shining on the other side of the world.

Even if you look at a light through a dirty window, it is our perception of the light, not the light itself that is hard to see clearly.

Jesus is the Light. Sometimes our perception of who He is might be made to look dim or dismal, because the view we are looking through has been tarnished. Or the curtain has been drawn, and we can't even see a flicker. But that doesn't change the fact of who He is, or what He came to do for us. I am here to tell you His light has not been snuffed out. If you cannot see His light, it is because you are still covered in a darkness of grief that keeps you from seeing it.

His light is constant. The hope He offers is constant. No matter the trials, no matter our darkness, no matter the depth of our suffocating pain.

No one is exempt from the effects of this fallen world we live in. Being a Christian is not a golden ticket to a perfect life. His faithfulness is not to stop anything bad from happening to us while we are in this world, but to hold us through the storms and hurricanes. He is even faithful to us when we are angry with Him and blaming Him for what happened.

Hope came as a gift in a manger. It came for *you*! Don't just let it sit there. Pick it up and unwrap it, and let His light of hope shatter your darkness.

Prayer: Jesus, I need the hope you came to bring. I need Your Light that shatters my darkness. No matter how long I have to wait, I will hold on, believing it is a gift that is on its way.

Day 6 – Friday

On Monday (day 2) I talked about perspective and how it affects our hope. While preparing this advent journey for all of us, I had an opportunity to personally experience this again.

Dave and I have a yearly tradition of booking a large condo at an indoor water park in Wisconsin Dells the week after Thanksgiving. He and I stay the whole week, and our (now adult) kids come and go (with our grandchildren) as their schedules permit. Some years the visits are short and we have quite a bit of time to ourselves; sometimes we have a fairly even mix of both, and there are some years we have kids and grandkids here the entire week.

I will admit to you that no matter how much I love my family, so much "togetherness" can get a bit overwhelming. I have discovered that many of us, after the death of our child, can't handle the chaos of young children, noise and crowds for any length of time. That has been the case for me even years later, which at times can be especially frustrating since I am by profession a preschool teacher and an international children's minister, and used to love that kind of atmosphere.

But this time, I was determined to have a good week and made a conscious decision to enjoy the busyness, noise and chaos. I decided to view it as the opportunity and blessing that it is, and not give in to the frustration that it can be.

What a difference that determined decision made! We had family with us all but one day, and before I knew it, our time was over and we were heading back home, full of wonderful memories.

I want to encourage you to do something similar with this Christmas season. Even if you don't think you can, make a determined effort to find ways to celebrate this time of year. Make sure the children around you have fun. Make a determined decision to find ways to celebrate and honor Christ, who is the giver of Hope!

It doesn't mean that every day will be better, but you will have many more good days than if you were living under the determined decision that it is impossible to enjoy anything about Christmas this year. (And that *is* something we are guilty of telling ourselves...)

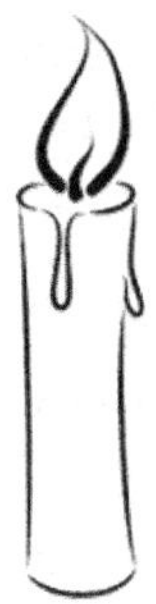

(LIGHT THE GREEN CANDLE)

When something is dried up, it can be seen as dead. But that isn't always the case. I think one way we could describe us as pareavors, is being in a drought. Our life has just dried up, and there is no life.

But think about what a drought often does. On top of the soil, what we see looks like death. But under the soil, where we can't see, drought makes a tree's roots grow very deep, which causes a strength and stability that cannot be gotten in any other way.

In Ezekiel 17:24, God tells us that He dries up the green tree *and* makes the dry tree flourish.

And remember Job 14: 7? "There is hope for a tree that has been cut down; it can come back to life and sprout" (GNT).

1 Peter 5:10 is another verse that gives me so much hope in the deep work God is doing. Paul prays that after we have suffered a while, God will bring us to a place of full maturity, establish us, strengthen us and set you and me on a more firm foundation than we have ever been on before.

According to Romans 5:1-5, we can be full of joy here and now even in our trials and troubles. Taken in the right spirit, these very things will give us patient endurance, which will develop a mature character, which produces a steady hope that will never disappoint us!

God is doing something so deep that it looks and feels like you have died. I know for a long time we want to die. But your draught will come to an end at some point, and there will be new life. You just have to wait for it. (There's that advent "waiting" thing again.)

If you want to do something toward helping yourself to not have a horrible Christmas season, may I suggest finding decorations with the word "hope" that you can put around your house. Literally surround yourself with HOPE!

And if you feel like you just don't have the hope you need right now to get through the holidays, you can lean on our hope until you have your own.

Pray: God, your Word says that hope deferred or misplaced, makes the heart sick, but when it has come to fullness, it brings life. I ask for You to plant a seed of hope that brings life into what looks like death in me. Amen.

Day 7 - Saturday

Light brings life. Think about it. Without light, there would be no life on this earth.

That is the case both physically and spiritually. "The light shines in the darkness, and the darkness did not comprehend it," John 1:5 (NKJV). In other words, the darkness could not overcome, put out, or extinguish the light.

The battle of this world is light against darkness. How do you get rid of darkness? You don't get rid of the darkness by removing it. You get rid of the darkness by turning on a light.

You can't get rid of the darkness in your life by removing it in some way. There is only one way. You *have* to bring the light of Jesus into the darkness in your life! And when you do that, the darkness begins to flee. It might not happen right away. It might come and go for a while, but if you keep bringing Jesus into your darkness, it *will* change the darkness into light. The enemy will fight it. But be persistent. Do whatever you can, whenever you can.

And guess what? Darkness cannot overpower light, but light will always shatter the darkness, which means the Light always wins.

(LIGHT THE GREEN CANDLE)

Isaiah 9:2-6 "The people who walk in darkness shall see a great Light—a Light that will shine on all those who live in the land of the shadow of death....For unto us a child is born, unto us a son is given..." (TLB).

Jesus is the light of the world. Jesus is your light. He is your life. He is your hope.

Hope is a key. What is the purpose of a key? It unlocks something. When we are locked out of our house or our car, we usually have to give someone a call to rescue us, to let us in to a place we have a right to be.

Jesus paid a very high price for us to be able to have certain gifts in our lives. Because we are in Christ, we have a right to have peace in Him. We have a right to have joy in Him. We have a right to have love in Him and all that love brings. But the death of our child causes us to feel locked out of having those things.

The reason I have become passionate about extending hope to pareavors is because there is so much out there from grieving parents who are stuck in their grief, telling other grieving parents their lives will always be dark, and life will never be worth living again without their child.

Way too many bereaved parents have remained locked up in that dark, hopeless place. Some of them don't want to come out, because they are afraid it means they will forget their child. It's easy to believe the pain we feel equals not forgetting them. At the same time, we want to stop hurting so much. Our minds are in so much turmoil and confusion.

Very early after Becca's death, I personally refused to believe that I was trapped in the suffocating darkness with no way out. I knew that my life would never be the same, but I could not come into agreement that it would always be dark and not worth living.

I had four other children and grandchildren. I had a calling on my life and an international ministry. I knew I had the Seed of Hope and Life living inside of me. As horrific as it was, I did not believe the death of my child was where God reached His limit, and He was unable to help me work through it to a place of peace and fulfillment. There had to be a way to honor my daughter with life, not more death.

Without hope, we can't move forward. That is true of anyone, but especially for grieving parents. We have been dealt such a huge blow, and as I have said, too many pareavors don't believe that hope is ever possible.

I don't want you to believe that, or to have to wait years for that glimmer of hope to reach you.

There is hope. Maybe you can't see that right now, but I am here to assure you that you can come out of your darkness and live again. You can have a productive life, enjoying the time you have left here on earth with your loved ones and friends.

Every pareavor I know who doesn't stay in that place of suffocating darkness for many years, is someone who reached out to God as their source of hope.

I pray you take the key of hope that I have been trying to hand to you for the last seven days, and allow it to unlock peace, joy and love back into your life as we continue our advent time.

And let me say it is okay to grieve. We will never get over missing our child; we will not reach a time here on earth where we are completely done grieving for the loss of our child. But we grieve with hope. The hope that the Christmas season celebrates.

Prayer: Tonight, pray your own prayer from your heart.

Week Two - PEACE

Day 1 - Sunday

(Start by lighting the green candle.)

All around the world, horrible things are happening. Horrible things have happened since the first murder, when a jealous man murdered his own brother. (I often wish God would have shared with us what it was like for Adam and Eve.)

When the birth of Jesus was announced by the angels, they proclaimed "peace on earth." God sent Himself, wrapped in a human body, so that His peace could walk around on earth in a time of turmoil. (The Jews were under Roman rule, and the Romans were known for their cruelty.)

Peace is God's plan. Peace came as a gift in the manger. What happened to that gift? The same thing that happened to God's perfect peace when time began. Sin happened; selfishness, cruelty, lust for power, jealousy.

But that doesn't keep God from continuing to offer His gift of peace. Just like I talked about the gift of hope, it is up to us to take it from Him and unwrap it for ourselves.

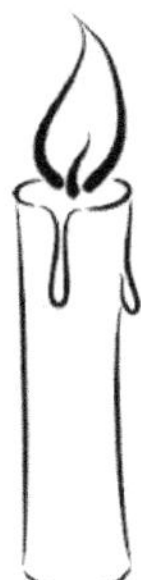

(LIGHT THE BLUE CANDLE)

Blue is the color I chose to represent peace in our advent journey, as it is known to be a peaceful color. If we think about it, beautiful calm blue water can put our soul at rest. Looking up at a beautiful blue sky (night or day) can make us feel at peace.

Jesus is called the Prince of Peace. When our child dies, it feels impossible to ever feel God's peace again. But that isn't the case.

God doesn't take His peace away from us. The enemy has stolen it from us, and sometimes we must fight to get it back. Paul talks about that in Hebrews 4:11 when he tells us to make every effort (some translations say to strive) to enter into the place of rest God has for us.

The battle can be fierce, but it makes the victory that much sweeter. When that peace comes, it is so satisfying, so pure, so beyond what we can understand!

One of our familiar Christmas songs says it well; "And in despair I bowed my head, there is no peace on earth I said. For hate is strong and mocks the song of peace on earth goodwill to men."

But the song then goes on to say, "then pealed the bells more loud and deep, God is not dead nor doth He sleep. The wrong shall fail, the right prevail, with peace on earth good will, to men." [1]

I said sometimes we have to fight to enter into a place of peace, but often, for those of us who are so shattered and broken hearted, quite often all we have to do is stop and rest, and that peace will come.

In other words, I can't make peace happen. But I can run into the arms of the One who can.

When Jesus died, the temple of the curtain in the Holy of Holies was torn in two. That was so we could come to God's throne boldly and find help in our time of need. It was also so that God did not have to stay behind a curtain, but could come out and love fully each individual He created.

That is what I want you to take a moment and do, right now. We are going to rest, not be angry, not fight, but rest in the arms and the presence of the One who loves you and wants to bring peace to your soul.

God has blessed us with the gift of imagination. For some reason, we "outgrow" it as adults (usually because we were taught that it is childish). I fully believe God wants us to use that gift for our entire time on earth. I am not talking about being "guided" by a spiritual being as those in the New Age movement do, but to be child-like in our faith, allowing the Holy Spirit to help us use our imagination as a springboard for what He wants to show us, or do for us.

Take a big breath, as if you are breathing in His gift of peace. As you breathe out, use your God-given imagination to picture stress leaving your body. Do it again, and as you breathe in, ask the Lord to come into your wounded soul to be your Prince of

Peace. As you breathe out, picture yourself giving Him the heaviness, the anger, etc.

Prayer: Prince of Peace, Your Word says that Your peace will guard our hearts and our minds. Help us to choose to come into alignment of that truth. Amen.

[1] (I Heard the Bells, taken from a poem of Henry Wadsworth Longfellow.) en.wikipedia.org/wiki/I_Heard_the_Bells_on_Christmas_Da

Day 2 - Monday

(Start by lighting the green candle.)

It may have looked like Jesus came as a sweet little baby, and He did. But he also came as a mighty King! We know He didn't come as an earthly king to overthrow an earthly government, but to overthrow Satan, the spiritual ruler of this world, and to nullify the eternal effects of the horrible things Satan puts in our individual lives while we are here on this earth.

Jesus is not a ruthless king, although we might think so after the death of our child. Yes, He came to right the wrongs, but not the way we often think. (Just like it wasn't the way the disciples thought.) He didn't come for a temporary earthly fix. He came to make things permanent, for all of eternity.

He is the Alpha and the Omega (Revelation 1:8) which means He is the beginning of all things and He is the end of all things. Not only does He have the final word, He IS the final Word!

I want you to think about this. Jesus, our King, has never lost a battle that He was brought into. His strategies will often be different than ours, and there may be times we don't like the playing field we find ourselves on, but when we bring Him into our battle, He *always* has the final Word, and the final victory!

There is a song that has been around for many years reminding us that sometimes He calms the storm, but other times He calms His child. Earthly kings might be able to control some physical things here and there, but only King Jesus can bring His Kingdom inside of us. For instance, He can bring peace to our shattered hearts. That is a much greater rule than any earthly king or kingdom!

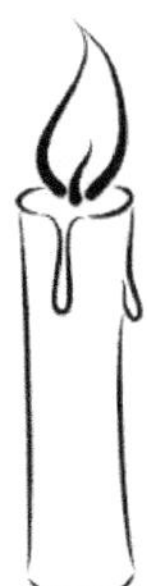

(LIGHT THE BLUE CANDLE)

Jesus wasn't just a baby. He isn't only a King to rule and reign. Jesus is also our shepherd.

John chapter ten talks about the thief (the enemy who is after the sheep) who comes to steal, kill, and destroy them. The enemy attacks the flock and scatters it.

But *we* have a good shepherd, Jesus, who will leave the ninety-nine sheep to go after the one sheep who has been attacked, and is lost and wounded. That would be you and me.

I talked about this last week with the theme of hope and the green candle. Psalm 23 says, "The Lord ADONAI is my shepherd... He has me lie down in grassy pastures, he leads me by quiet water, and he restores my inner person (my soul)" (CJB).

Hebrews 13 talks about how the God of peace, who through the blood of the eternal covenant, brought back from the dead our Lord Jesus, the great Shepherd of the sheep. What a wonderful thing He has done. We are in a blood covenant with Jesus, our shepherd, to provide peace for us whenever we need it.

And the best part is that it doesn't matter how far away you are from God in your anger or unforgiveness; God has peace for you. How do I know this? He tells us in Isaiah 57:19 and Ephesians 2:17 that there is peace to those both far and near.

How about another promise from the One who has the final word? Jeremiah 33:6 states, "I will heal my people and will let them enjoy abundant peace." He *will* heal your wounded shattered heart. Maybe not as soon as we want, and not even a complete healing here on this earth, but He will do it!

Luke 1:79 tells us that Jesus came to shine on those living in darkness and in the shadow of death, to guide our feet into the path of peace.

Jesus is our shepherd, to guide us into a place of peace; a peace that doesn't make any sense after the death of our child. But their death isn't the end, it is not the final word.

Peace is being extended to us. Our part is to let go of what we are carrying that keeps us from accepting His gift of peace. It is an exchange. We give Him our fear, anger, doubts, bitterness and so on, and He gives us peace. Sounds like a pretty good deal on our end!

Most of us are familiar with the promise in the book of Revelation about God wiping away all of our tears. But did you know it is because He is our shepherd? It is found in chapter 7, verse 17 and says, "For the Lamb at the center of the throne will be their shepherd; he will lead them to springs of living water. And God will wipe away every tear from their eyes," (NIV).

Prayer: Jesus, thank You for having the final word in my child's life and in my life. And thank You that one of those final words is peace for my life. Help me to let go of the things that are keeping me from accepting that gift of peace. Amen.

Day 3 - Tuesday

(Start by lighting the green candle.)

The enemy brings accusations and false blame. He causes chaos and confusion. It's almost like he is scrambling the frequency of what we need from God. So, we have to find the dial, and readjust the tuner.

Peace isn't something we just stumble upon in our turmoil. Psalm 34:14 & 1 Peter 3:11 both tell us to seek peace and pursue it. James 4:8 tells us to draw near to God and He will draw near to us. It isn't that God has left us, but that we can't feel His nearness.

The first instruction to us in that verse is to resist the devil. We are not resisting him when we remain in our anger and unforgiveness with God. Instead, we are adding fuel to the devil's fire.

Job lost seven children all at once. He also lost all his finances, and he lost his health with having big oozing boils. His wife told him to just curse God and die. His friends kept insisting he must have done something wrong for God to do this to him. All Job could say is, "I don't know why all of this has happened. But no matter how miserable I am, even if He kills me, I will trust Him". (Job 13, my paraphrase). He also said, "The Lord gives and the Lord takes away. Blessed be the name of the Lord," Job 21:1 (CSB).

That is an incredible trust in God; allowing God to be God, and recognizing that there is no way our finite minds can make sense of it. If we could figure out and make sense of everything God does and allows, He wouldn't be big enough to be God anymore, would He?

(LIGHT THE BLUE CANDLE)

We seem to believe if we let God off the hook, we won't have peace, but it is really just the opposite. I often picture a little child who was told "no" to something. That child starts to cry and throw a fit, sometimes hurting themselves in the process. The loving father steps in and scoops up the child who is now fighting *him* fiercely.

Eventually the child wears out, and receives the loving embrace and comfort of the father.

That is a pretty good picture of some of us, isn't it?

Romans 14:19 tells us to make every effort we can, to do what leads to peace. And often that means simply submitting to the embrace of our loving Father like Job tells us to do (Job 22:11); to submit to God and be at peace with Him.

For some reason, many of us think that being a Christian is a golden ticket to not have anything bad happen to us for the rest of our time here on earth. But that just isn't the case. We *are* going to deal with pain and suffering in this life because we live in a fallen sinful world, which means we need to learn what God's Word has to say about it, and how to deal with it, so that *when* it comes, our faith isn't shattered and we fall apart and blame God!

Are you thinking it's too late, because that has already happened? It is never too late to become firm in our trust in God to receive His peace.

Matthew 7:24-25 is where Jesus talks about the house built on the rock and on the sand. There are many of us who thought we had built our lives on the rock. But when our child died, we discovered it was on the sand, because everything came crashing down in a way that caused us to blame God, instead of giving our suffocating darkness and pain over to Him to heal our broken, shattered hearts.

Over the years, I have learned my faith is not in getting the answer I want to my prayer; my faith is knowing intimately the one to whom I pray! And the more I truly *know* Him the *more I trust* Him.

You might be shocked by that statement, because you may feel like you trusted God and He betrayed you, so you can never trust Him again. But the truth is, He is the source of hope and He is the source of peace, no matter what has happened in our lives.

And, t isn't just true for me. It is true for thousands of parents who have lost their child from this earth over the years.

Prayer: God, you tell us Psalm 29:11 that you bless Your people with peace. I thank you that I am truly blessed, because you made a way for me to have peace in the absolute worst storm possible. Amen.

Day 4 - Wednesday

(Start by lighting the green candle.)

Shalom! That is the Hebrew word for peace. It means a state of rest, quietness and calmness, tranquility, harmonious relationships between God and men; a state of wholeness.

In other words, the repairing of a shattered heart.

When an angel appeared to someone in the Bible, they would often start their message with the word, "Peace!". There were also several times when Jesus appeared to His disciples that He also started by speaking peace over them.

When Peter, John and Jude wrote their letters that became books in the New Testament, six times they started out by speaking God's peace over those in the church reading their letters.

In counting how often Paul often started his letters to the churches by speaking peace to the readers, I discovered that twelve of them started with "grace and peace." Four times, he also ended his letter by speaking a word of peace over his fellow believers.

In the book of Psalms, we are told how the Lord delights in the peace of his people (Psalm 35:27). That means He takes pleasure in our wholeness and well-being.

You may be thinking, "If that is true, then why did he allow my child to die?" I am not God. I don't have an answer to that. And most of us probably won't get an answer this side of life. But I *can* tell you He wants to give you peace.

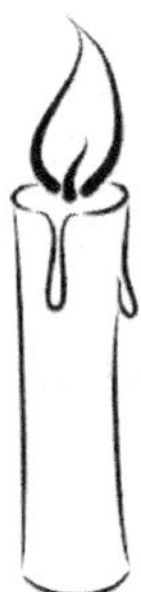

(LIGHT THE BLUE CANDLE)

Jesus didn't come to this earth as a baby to grow up and sacrifice His life so that nothing bad would ever happen to us on this earth. He died so we would have a way to be connected to Him while on this earth. He died so we could have hope, and so that we could have peace.

The "no more tears" part is *after* we leave this world. If God were to be our magic genie, and we could get whatever we want from him, people would just use Him. It would not be a relationship built on love and trust. Trust is believing in someone when things don't make sense.

Isaiah 53:5 says the chastisement for us to have peace was placed on Him. He was punished, so that we could have peace, and could receive healing from His wounds. He was beaten, so we could be whole. He was whipped, so we could be healed. He suffered, as a way to take our burdens and replace it with peace.

That is why Paul seems to put grace and peace together so often. Because God's incredible grace is His divine empowerment to be able to receive His Shalom. His wholeness. His peace. Through the death of His own son.

So, let's extend this peace just a bit further.

One of the times Jesus Himself spoke peace directly over his followers is John 20:21, "Peace be with you! As the Father has sent me, I am sending you" (NIV).

That makes me think of a question. What is God sending *you* to do, in your child's honor? What can you go and do, that will bring life to your child and to you, by keeping their memory alive? What can you do, that will help bring in a measure of peace that your child's life matters, and he or she will continue to live on, even though they are no longer here on this earth?

"Grace and peace to you from the One who is, and who was, and who is to come," Revelation 1:4 (CSB). This tells me that an eternal God had you covered in the area of peace before your child, or you, were even born.

He paid the highest price possible, the death of His child, so that you could have peace and wholeness within the death of your own child.

Prayer: Holy Spirit, I come into agreement with God's Word and speak God's peace (His wholeness) over myself. I speak peace over my family and peace in my home, and that this peace will remain through the rest of this Christmas season. Amen.

Day 5 - Thursday

(Start by lighting the green candle.)

There are so many scriptures that link Jesus to peace. The apostle Paul tells us in Ephesians 2:14 that Jesus himself is our peace.

There are also times Jesus links Himself directly to peace. We see that in John 14:27 when He tells us, "I give you peace, the kind of peace that only I can give. It isn't like the peace that this world can give," (CEV). And another time He very bluntly shares, "I have told you these things, so that in me you may have peace. In this world, you will have trouble. But take heart! I have overcome the world," John 16:33 (NIV).

This time of year, especially, we are reminded that Jesus is called the Prince of Peace.

Isaiah 9:6 seems to be everywhere, including a main theme for Christmas cards. "For to us a child is born... And he will be called ...Prince of Peace," (NKJV).

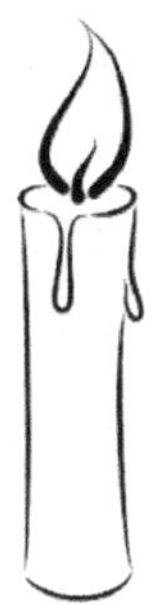

(LIGHT THE BLUE CANDLE)

Often, especially in Biblical times, a prince was known to lead the battles of a war. He was proving his leadership ability to eventually take over the throne and earning the trust and loyalty of the people of his future kingdom.

In this context, the title, Prince of Peace, means that He is leading the battle for our peace. Every war has many battles. Jesus is the only King who wins every battle He enters, which means He also wins the war. Part of His victory happens by helping us defeat the enemy in our personal battles.

Romans 16:20 promises that the God of peace will crush Satan under *our* feet. His peace in our lives is part of the battle plan. It is a valuable weapon we need, to win the battle of darkness we have found ourselves thrown into.

Jesus Himself made sure we had access to this powerful weapon of peace, by purchasing it for us at a very high price; the Prince of Peace sacrificed His own life for it.

Then there is God the Father. He paid what we as bereaved parents might consider the ultimate price for us to have peace; He turned His son over to men to die a very torturous death.

God knows what it is like to have a child die! He allowed Himself to feel the deepest pain possible, so that *we* could have peace from the burdens of this world whenever we need it, including the death of our own child.

The bottom line is that our Father God willingly sacrificed His child, so that we could have peace within the death of our child. It is an exchange. He exchanged His son, the Prince of Peace, for our pain, confusion and turmoil, to give us the peace we so desperately need.

Last night, we talked about Isaiah 53 that says He was beaten so that we could have peace, and we receive healing from His wounds. We see that in the New Testament as well, after Jesus died. Romans 5:1 and Colossians 1:20 confirm that Jesus paid the price for our peace through His death on the cross.

What an incredible, amazing thought; Jesus left the glory of heaven to come to earth as a baby for the purpose of dying, so that we could have peace in our suffocating darkness! It doesn't make sense, does it? But Jesus made what seems impossible become possible.

You may be thinking, "That sounds great, and it works for you, but I don't have that peace. How can I get it?"

You receive it as the gift that it is. Just like salvation. We start by laying down the things that cause the darkness in our lives, so we have empty hands to receive. Remember, it is an exchange. You might have to let go of anger, guilt or blame. Let it go as best as you can, so you can offer the Prince of Peace room in your heart for the peace He is waiting to give you. And let me acknowledge, it may be simple, but not always easy.

Prayer: Holy Spirit, help me to let go of the things I need to let go of, to be able to receive Your gift. Father God, may the price you paid, the death of Your Son, not be in vain. Prince of Peace, I accept the weapon You battled for me to have, a peace that goes beyond understanding. Amen.

Day 6 - Friday

(Start by lighting the green candle.)

How is it that the pain of our child who is gone from this earth outweighs the desire to stay for the ones we still have here?

We see something similar in a story Jesus shared with us. It is the shepherd who left to go find the lost sheep. The shepherd had ninety-nine of his sheep with him, but left them all to go after the one.

Obviously, we can't go after our child and bring him or her back. But I believe it shows us that it is okay to have the focus of our pain outweigh the blessing of those we still have... for a while. But there does come a point where we need to start getting our focus back on the ninety-nine, realizing "the one" isn't really lost, but safely with the Shepherd and patiently waiting for us to join him or her.

For many of us, that focus is our other children. If we don't have other children (and I am so sorry if that is the case for you), then it is our spouse or other family members and/or friends who still need us in their lives.

My younger daughter came to me several months after Becca died, and told me she thought I wished it was her that died instead of her sister. That totally shocked me, but I found out that is a very common belief of the surviving siblings. They interpret our deep pain and inability to function as, "the wrong one died."

So, if you are not interested in having peace for your own sake (you *want* to stay mad at God and blame Him), maybe you should consider releasing that hostility and darkness for the sake of your other children, or for those who love you and need you.

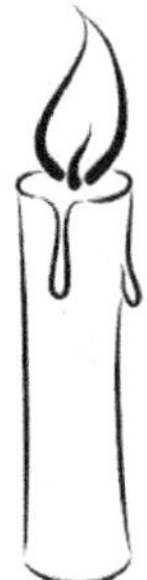

(LIGHT THE BLUE CANDLE)

Some people think peace is feeling good about a situation. I have found that peace is resting in God, in spite of the situation. It is a belief that God is going to come through and somehow things are going to be okay.

You might be thinking, "How can things possibly be okay when my child has died?" I completely understand. (Remember, I have been there...)

God's ways are beyond what we can understand. If they weren't, He wouldn't be big enough to be God. That also means that His attributes, like His peace, are beyond what we can understand.

There are people who say God won't ever give us more than we can handle. You will not find that in the Bible anywhere. He says in 1 Corinthians 10:13 that we won't be tempted more than what we can handle and will always make a way of escape for us, but that is not the same thing. In fact, we are told just the opposite, like in 2 Corinthians chapter twelve, where we read that His power is made the strongest in our weakness.

Those of us who have lost a child, know this *is* more than we can handle. And it is in this place of suffocating darkness that we know just how weak we are and how much we need Him to be our hope, our light, and to be our peace. And that is often where we have a huge struggle. We know in our heads that we need Him, but our emotions are not lining up with those thoughts.

We may think the battle is won in our emotions, but fighting there is a losing battle. The battle we need to win is in our thoughts, because it is our shift in perspective that allows the peace to come through, eventually overcoming the negative emotions that keep peace from reaching us.

Isaiah 26:3 is very clear that when our minds are steadfast, we have peace. "You will keep the mind that is dependent on You in perfect peace," (HCSB). Romans 8:6 reminds us that the mind governed by the flesh (our emotions) is death, but the mind governed by the Spirit is life and peace.

In other words, it really is up to us. We can choose to believe the thoughts of our emotions or the thoughts of our spirit. And based on our choice, we will either bear the fruit of our flesh, which are things like confusion, anger and bitterness, or we will bear the fruit of the Spirit, one of which is peace. (See Galatians 5:22.) And when we have the fruit of peace activated in our lives, according to Isaiah 32:17 its effect will be quietness and rest in our souls.

In my prayer room, I have a saying taped to my desk that says, "Peace comes from the presence of God. Not the absence of trouble." Last week, we talked about how you don't get rid of darkness by taking it away. You get rid of it by bringing in the light. It is the same with peace. You don't get rid of turmoil and confusion by taking it away. You get rid of it by receiving God's peace.

Don't be discouraged if this doesn't happen as quickly as you want it to. It is a process. Stick with it, and you will eventually find yourself walking and living from a place of peace.

Prayer: Lord, I choose Your Spirit of peace over my desires of the flesh that leads me down a path of darkness and pain. I give my mind to You. And I thank You that the truth will always set me free. Amen.

Day 7 - Saturday

(Start by lighting the green candle.)

When Jesus was born, the angels announced to a group of shepherds that the birth of this special baby was the good news of God's peace coming to earth. What the angels didn't announce, was the huge price tag attached to that peace. Bringing God's peace to this earth wasn't going to be an easy road for that little baby, or His Father who sent Him here.

On Thursday, I said that simple doesn't always mean easy. Peace doesn't always mean easy, either. Being a Christian doesn't mean we will have smooth sailing here on earth.

Jesus never promised us an easy life. (As a note, when Jesus said in Matthew 11:30 that His yoke was easy and His burden was light, it was in the context of rules, traditions and the judgments of man in the form of religious bondage.)

In fact, we have been told to *expect* tribulation (John 16:33) and trials (James 1:2). Jesus warned us to build our lives on the solid Rock, so that *when* (not if) the winds blew, the rains fell and the flood waters rose, we would be able to stay standing.

No, He certainly did not promise life here would be easy. But what He *did* promise is to walk with us (Matthew 12:20), to never leave us or abandon us (Hebrews 13:5), and to be our source of strength (Ephesians 3:16). He also said that if we called on Him, He would give us God's peace; the same peace the angels announced at His birth and that He paid the full price for, which goes beyond our comprehension (Philippians 4:6-7).

(LIGHT THE BLUE CANDLE)

Sometimes, instead of moving toward God's light and giving Him our pain, as pareavors, we try to stay in control. We try hard to make our own safe little world so nothing else will happen. But that won't bring peace, because it is impossible to be in control of everything. I think of how the government is constantly passing new laws to "make us safe." But there is no way there can be enough laws to make us completely and totally safe. There is no way you can have all the control, so that nothing else bad will happen in your life.

At this point, the safest thing we can do is to lean into God as much as possible. Climb up on His lap as your Daddy. Let Him wrap His arms of love around you like a blanket that warms your heart. If you can't feel His presence or His peace, ask God to heighten your awareness of Him. Think of the words in a familiar Christmas song, "Be near me, Lord Jesus, I ask you to stay, close by me forever..." Let these words be the cry of your heart.

In the Old Testament, after the temple had been destroyed and it was being rebuilt, God declared, "In this place I will grant peace" (Haggai 2:9). We are now the temple of God's Spirit. We have been destroyed with the death of our child, and we desperately need to be rebuilt. And I believe God is declaring the same words over His temple; over you and over me. "In this place, I will grant peace!"

I am not saying you will eventually be rebuilt and get back to your old self, because that will never happen. But I am saying you can have peace as you are learning how to live with your child no longer here on earth, and while you are finding your new identity that goes beyond being a parent whose child has died. (I felt for quite some time that my identity was being a mom whose daughter died, until I learned how to live in an identity that honored the life of my daughter, instead of living in the shadow of her death.)

And having peace does not mean the pain will automatically leave. Many Christians have the false belief that if you are grieving or in pain (physically or emotionally), it is because you aren't giving that thing to God, or you "don't have enough faith." One surprising thing I have learned is that peace and pain can reside together in me. We don't have to choose between leaning on God or falling apart. We can lean on God *while* we fall apart, allowing Him to give us that miraculous peace that goes beyond our understanding. And it's okay that it doesn't make sense. I am just thankful He paid the price for it to be possible.

"Now may the Lord of peace himself give you peace at all times and in every way. The Lord be with all of you," 2 Thessalonians 3:16 (NIV).

Prayer: Father, I know You have done Your part in making a way for me to have peace that goes beyond any possible understanding. Help me to do my part; to let go of anything that keeps me from leaning on You, and allowing You to grant peace in me, Your temple. Amen.

Week Three - JOY

Day 1 - Sunday

(Start by lighting the green and blue candles.)

I am not about to tell you that losing your child will turn into something joyous in your life. But I will tell you it is possible to have joy again in your life, beyond the grief.

My joy is different now than it used to be.

How is that possible? There isn't more than one kind of joy, is there? No, I don't believe there is.

I believe what has happened to me, is that my joy is more of a solid undercurrent in my life now. It is built into the foundation and very fiber of my being. It has become a rock on which I am anchored.

True joy is not based on outward circumstances which can go away if those circumstances change, nor is it some euphoric happiness. It is based on a constant inner knowing of truth, beyond the outward circumstances. It is an undercurrent of contentment, confidence, and that seed of hope that has been planted and is now growing and bearing fruit in my life.

(LIGHT THE YELLOW CANDLE)

God has graciously given us many keys to unlock doors of truth that will help us, while here on earth. Sometimes those keys seem to be handed to us, and other times it seems we need to look for them... on our hands and knees... in the dark.

The death of our child seems to be one of those times of searching for keys in the darkness of a moonless night.

However, the Holy Spirit has given us a clue to at least one of the keys to unlock and release joy back into our lives. That key is choosing to be thankful. Now don't go tuning me out, not yet!

Whatever we focus on will consume us. If my thoughts and focus remain on my loss, the torment and pain of it will consume me. If my thoughts and focus are on the blessings I still have, thankfulness will begin to awaken a joy that has gone dormant inside of me.

Once again, this is something we choose to do, not based on our emotions or how we feel, but based on the truth of who God is.

It is *not* impossible, no matter where you are in this grief journey. Start with the smallest things. Those who have never lost a child will tell us to start with thanking God that we are breathing, or that we woke up today. In the early days and months, that isn't something most of us are thankful for, because we don't want to be here on this earth any more. But that does not mean there isn't anything to be thankful for.

What about the fact that you *have* a bed to sleep in? You probably own a phone that allows you to connect with people when you want and need to (and can turn off when you don't). Who helped you plan the funeral in all of your numbness and pain? Did anyone bring you and your family food when you didn't have it in you to cook? Do you have a pet that is keeping you company? How about a TV that you can sit in front of and zone out when you can't sleep? Did you remember where you parked your car coming out of the store the last time you went? The things we pareavors can find to be thankful for may be a strange list to everyone else, and that is okay!

If you do it consciously and consistently, you will find a spark of hope igniting. Keep going, and it will turn into light, and life.

Even if you don't feel it, you can speak your words of thanks to a God who made sure this wasn't the end, but just a transfer into the beginning of something so wonderful it cannot even be fully described!

"But let me tell you something wonderful, a mystery I'll probably never fully understand...In the resurrection scheme of things, this has to happen: everything perishable taken off the shelves and replaced by the imperishable, this mortal replaced by the immortal. Then the saying will come true: death swallowed by triumphant Life! Who got the last word, oh, death? Oh, death, who's afraid of you now? It was sin that made death so frightening and law-code guilt that gave sin its leverage, its destructive power. But now in a single victorious stroke of Life, all three—sin, guilt, death—are gone, the gift of our Master, Jesus Christ. THANK GOD! (1 Corinthians 15:56-58 MSG)

Prayer: Jesus, thank You that this is not permanent, and that You really do have the final word over death. Help us to understand how powerful our thoughts are, and to find things to be thankful for, knowing we need this key to unlock ourselves from the chains of death that are holding us tightly bound in darkness. Amen.

Day 2 - Monday

(Start by lighting the green and blue candles.)

At first, the thought of getting further and further away from Becca could put me into a tailspin. But one day, God graciously reminded me that I was not getting further away from her, but closer to her. It is all in my perspective.

If I am thinking of my earthly loss and how her life gets further away from me as time goes by, things become very heavy and difficult. If I am thinking of my eternal home, the truth is that every day I am getting closer to seeing her again. So, in reality, I am not getting farther away from her, but each day that I am here on earth means I am one day closer to her!

I will readily admit that it isn't always easy to make this shift in my thoughts. As parents, we are supposed to leave this earth before our children. I still want her here with me now, and it hurts that she isn't here with us, especially during special family days and holidays.

I have found that a shift in my perspective (how I view and think about Becca's death) can make one of the biggest differences in how I deal with the grief of her being gone.

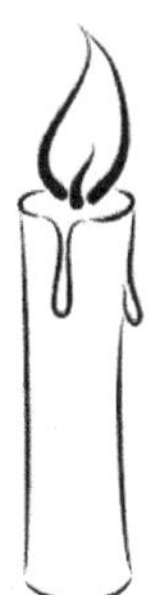

(LIGHT THE YELLOW CANDLE)

Let's do what the shepherds did in Luke 2:18-20. Let's take time to wonder at the birth of Jesus; to ponder and think about its meaning. Not just in general, but what does that mean for you and me personally, this Christmas season and for the rest of our time here on earth?

Let's think about why Jesus came to earth so many years ago, giving up the splendor of heaven to come here to our sinful world full of pain and suffering. Why would he do that? Why would He leave His "God powers" behind, and live as a man, dependent on the Holy Spirit living inside of Him?

For those of us who have lost a child, those answers will be from a totally different perspective of things than the rest of the world.

Do you know why I chose a yellow candle for joy? Yes, yellow is a color that stands for happiness, and it makes people feel more upbeat.

But yellow is also the color for light, and we need to be reminded that even though the light of our soul may have gone out, the light of His spirit inside of us will never go out. Jesus came for that very reason; so that the same Spirit who lived inside of Him, guiding and comforting Him while on earth, could also live inside us, to guide and comfort us for our time here. Not from some "out there somewhere" place, but directly inside of us. He isn't just Emmanuel, God *with* us, He is God *in* us! That boggles my mind when I take time to really think about it.

His light and His strength inside of us, is what will get us through the darkness and back to a place of light, where joy can break through in our lives once again.

If you are anything like me, Christmas used to be one of my favorite times of year because of the fun we have together as a family, and how much I like to make it fun for the children in my life. But that is another area we can make a shift in our thoughts, that will help us within our darkness and pain.

As pareavors, we may all lose our *desire* to celebrate, but we never lose our *reason*, which is to acknowledge the day Jesus came into this world to make a way for us to be together with our children again forever. The reason for Christmas is not to celebrate our children, but to celebrate the One who gave our children life, entrusted us with them for their short time on earth, and then made a way for us to be together for all of eternity.

Allow yourself to be in awe of the purpose of His life, His death, His time in the grave and His resurrection. All of that was to keep us from suffering the *final* effects of sin and death. Because He lives, our child still lives! And because He was resurrected from death to life, and lives inside of us, we can also raise up from our own death in our souls to life once again, here on this earth.

Prayer: Father, thank You for sending Jesus to this earth. Thank You for the plan you had in place to reunite me with my child before either one of us was even born. Help me to see Christmas through Your eyes of love more than my eyes of pain. Amen.

Day 3 - Tuesday

(Start by lighting the green and blue candles.)

A very important benefit of Christianity is the tremendous sense of identity we have that comes from knowing Jesus Christ in a very personal way. As we grow in knowing Him, we grow in that identity. We grow in knowing how much God loves us, and how each one of us are created uniquely, for a special purpose.

When our child dies, it can make us feel like that identity has been lost; that we only *thought* we knew who God was, and that if He really did create us for a special purpose, He was very cruel in that purpose.

Families also give us a sense of identity and purpose. Once again, when our child leaves this earth before we do, it shatters our sense of identity as a parent and our purpose in that role (even if we have other children).

I don't know about you, but I have had other tragedies happen in my life, before Becca died. Each time something happens, it is easy to ask God why He allowed it in our lives.

As I have looked back at those other painful events, I can see God's hand in it, which I couldn't see in the middle of the crisis. Looking back, we can often connect the dots and see how God used that situation to bring needed direction we might not have even known we needed, or to bring someone we love into a needed place of healing or restoration.

For instance, when Dave graduated college with a Computer Science degree, he felt led not to relocate, but it took a few months for a job to open up to him in our area. And that job was with a non-profit organization, so the pay was miserably low. However, they did make up for it in insurance benefits, which at the time was not a big deal to us. But God knew that within the next few months, we would need those benefits. That was when Becca (who was only three years old at the time) was diagnosed with cancer, had her leg amputated, and went through nine months of chemotherapy. During that time, her medical bills were easily in the hundreds of thousands, but we only had to cover less than $1000 that whole time!

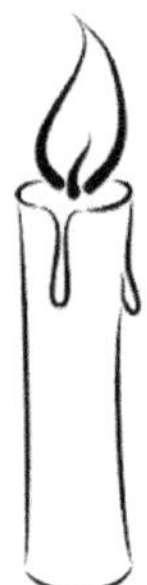

(LIGHT THE YELLOW CANDLE)

Can you think of a time where something bad happened, and looking back, it was really God working something out for good down the road that you couldn't see?

Based on that, let me gently make a suggestion. Many times, when we are saying, "God, why did you let this happen to me?" His answer might be, "I didn't let it happen *to* you. I let it happen *for* you."

You may be ready to throw this book across the room thinking, "There is no way I can listen to this and have Laura tell me the death of my child was something God did *for* me!"

And I am not about to say that!

Remember, I have been in that place of suffocating darkness myself, and have told God to just kill me now and take me off this earth. I am not going to tell you that God allowed your child to die, as something good He did for you.

We all know our lives will never be the same. *We* will never be the same. But within that, we can allow the death of our child to not be wasted. We can allow God's love to wash over us, to heal us, and to take the change in us and use it against the enemy who brought death into this world.

Although it hurts so much we just want to die and go to be with our child, the fact is, our child is safe in His arms. Our child does not have to face the pain and crap and tragedies this world puts us through. (And if that is something you question or that torments you because you don't know if that's true, go back and read Week One, Day One where I talk about that.)

When we think of our loss, our pain makes it hard to even breathe. When we think of our child's gain, it lifts some of that suffocating darkness, and allows us to see a glimmer of hope, and the possibility that maybe God isn't as cruel as we thought He was, and that we can live again and actually even find some happiness in our lives.

Prayer: God, I don't understand why You allowed my child to die, and I probably never will while here on this earth. Help me to not blame You for my pain, but the enemy who brought death into this world. Help me to begin to think more about my child's gain more than my loss. Amen.

Day 4 - Wednesday

(Start by lighting the green and blue candles.)

I may be broken into what feels like a million pieces, but I don't want to be destroyed by this. I don't want to just survive; I want to learn how to thrive again. Is that even possible? Does it make any sense?

Last night, I ended by saying it is possible to find happiness in our lives once again. I also believe it is totally possible to have joy again. You might be thinking, "Is there a difference?" Yes, there is.

As I said before, happiness is a good feeling based on outward circumstances, and that feeling can go away if those circumstances change. God's meaning of joy is not some euphoric feeling. It is a peace that comes from an underlying belief that God is in control, and that I can rejoice in His goodness and faithfulness at work in my life, even when I can't see it or feel the effects of it at the moment.

Joy is based on a constant inner knowing of truth, beyond the outward circumstances. But that doesn't mean I don't feel deep pain or sorrow along with it.

I think perhaps happiness is a feeling in our soul, and joy is a knowing in our spirit. The scriptural basis for this can be found in Galatians 5:22, which tells us that one of the fruits of the Spirit in our lives is joy. So, the Holy Spirit produces joy in us, based on our allowing Him to be at work in our lives. And where would that be? In our spirits, since we connect with God spirit-to-spirit.

Happiness = soul fruit; Joy = spiritual fruit.

(LIGHT THE YELLOW CANDLE)

Once again, joy is not a feeling that is based on the outward circumstances, but an inward knowing that God still has blessings for us that we don't yet know about. He truly is for us, not against us. It is a "knowing" that runs beside peace, which goes beyond anything we can understand. Joy is what causes us to delight in His mercy and grace in our lives, within the horrible earthly loss. It is the stirring of hope that this is *not* final, and we *will* see our child again.

I have noticed that in the Bible, peace and joy often seem to go together.

- Those who promote peace will have joy. (Proverbs 12:20)
- You will go out in joy and be led in peace. (Isaiah 55:12)
- The kingdom of God is not a matter of eating and drinking (a physical kingdom), but it is righteousness, peace and joy in the Holy Spirit. (Romans 14:17)
- The God of hope wants to fill you with joy and peace as you trust in Him, so that you may overflow with hope by the power of the Holy Spirit. (Romans 15:13)

I want to share with you the words of another parent.

> *After almost 7 years from the loss of our (son), joy can coexist with sorrow and you can respectfully live with both! We think of (son) every day, I think of him every second of every day, but for us we can very clearly see the one set of footprints where He carried us! We are beginning to celebrate his life with love and laughter and that's good! We have missed that! I think my healing may take a lifetime; I'm a mom, but what I know is that as I walk through this journey I will embrace the joy and the tears, I will embrace the happy and the sad! I have two children, one lives in Heaven, the other lives here with me, and my heart abides with both! (Come Grieve Through Our Eyes)*

Yes, joy and happiness are two different things, but we can have both again eventually. Here is something another pareavor wrote, to encourage you.

> *JOY was something I thought would never be in my life again after my 19 year old daughter died 14 years ago, I struggled for 10 years ... then one day I made the decision to finally start moving forward... I bought stocking hangers that spelled out JOY, a friend gave me a coffee cup that had the word JOY on it, it seemed the word JOY was everywhere I looked... What I did not realize was that JOY was all around me, I saw it in my son, I saw it in my work, and finally I saw it in myself. Joy is hard to achieve, you have to work at being happy, JOY is harder than grief... don't wait 10 years cause now I sometimes think I wasted some of those years but for me it took me that long. My son got married 2 years ago and they needed Christmas decorations so I went thru mine and I gave them my JOY stocking hangers ... I had to laugh at myself and said I'm giving away my JOY!!!!... (Come Grieve Through Our Eyes)*

You may think that joy is something you will never have in your life again, especially at Christmas time. But I assure you, that does not need to be the case. It may take a long time - a few years even - but you can have both joy and happiness once again, if you make the choice when it presents itself.

Prayer: Father, I have a hard time seeing my future with joy and happiness. Help me to allow the Holy Spirit to grow the fruit of joy in me, and to not shut the door on future happiness. Amen.

Day 5 - Thursday

(Start by lighting the green and blue candles.)

I have already talked about thankfulness being a key to unlock joy in our lives once again. There are a couple more keys I want to share with you tonight.

The first one is reaching out to others. God began putting other moms in my life who had recently lost their child. One was a distant friend whose son died six months after Becca, and the services were in the same funeral home. I don't know how, but I found myself standing in line for the visitation. When this mom and I hugged, and I told her how very sorry I was, she began to cry, knowing someone was holding her who could understand the depth of her loss. (I will admit, I didn't have it in me to stay for the funeral.)

Obviously, that was not a joyful event. But it helped unlock the door to joy, even though I didn't realize it at the time. I have discovered that every time I can strengthen, offer hope, or help someone else in some way, it opens the door wider for more joy to be released. It is God's law of sowing and reaping. Giving is a spiritual act that bears spiritual fruit.

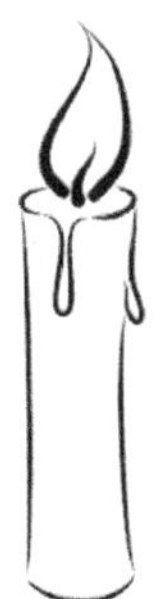

(LIGHT THE YELLOW CANDLE)

God says our grief can turn to joy. "You will be sorrowful, but your sorrow will be turned into joy," (John 16:20 - NIV) is just one of many scriptures with a promise of mourning and sorrow being turned into joy in our lives. I choose to believe His Word, no matter what my feelings tell me at the moment. I choose to plant a seed of hope and watch it grow, being watered by His promises, and become the fruit of joy manifested in my life.

And that is the other key I want to share with you. Several years ago, I started praying for joy to have a stronger presence in my life. (Okay, there was an extra key just tossed in if you caught it.) God led me to look up and write out eight pages of scriptures about joy and read through some of them every day for quite some time. I discovered being immersed in the Word of God on the subject of joy was pretty powerful.

I know some of you have no desire to crack your Bible open. I understand. So, I am going to share just a few of those verses here for you to read. (All of them are taken from the NIV.)

> *1 Chronicles 16:27 Splendor and majesty are before him; strength and joy are in his dwelling place.*
>
> *Job 33:26 ...they will see God's face and shout for joy; he will restore them to full well-being.*
>
> *Psalm 30:11 You turned my wailing into dancing; you removed my sackcloth and clothed me with joy.*
>
> *Psalm 51:12 Restore to me the joy of your salvation and grant me a willing spirit, to sustain me.*
>
> *Psalm 86:4 Bring joy to your servant, Lord, for I put my trust in you.*
>
> *Isaiah 51:11 They will enter Zion with singing; everlasting joy will crown their heads. Gladness and joy*

will overtake them, and sorrow and sighing will flee away.

Isaiah 61:3 ...to bestow on them a crown of beauty instead of ashes, the oil of joy instead of mourning, and a garment of praise instead of a spirit of despair. They will be called oaks of righteousness, a planting of the LORD for the display of his splendor.

I hope you take time to meditate on these. Read them silently. Read them out loud. Take a few words at a time and think about what those words mean for your life and how you can apply them.

Remember, these things are not done based on how we feel, but on the truth of who God is. The feelings will follow our meditation on the truth of His Word, and being in His presence. If my focus is on the loss, I will continue to be consumed by grief, pain and torment. If my thoughts and focus are on the blessings I have, thankfulness and joy will rise up and eventually consume me.

The goal is not to eliminate the grief. That will never happen. I have friends whose children have been gone for thirty or forty years. (My mind can't grasp that.) They still get hit with waves of grief at certain times, including unexpected times that take them by surprise. The goal is to allow God to work in our lives to bring a measure of healing which will allow us to function and live in a way that honors the life of our son or daughter; to have a life that is fulfilling and joyful until we are reunited with them and can hear the words, "Well done, good and faithful servant."

Prayer: Jesus, I surrender to You and Your miracle working ways. I want to live from a place of Truth. I ask You to bring hope, confidence and contentment back into my life. And I thank You that when I have those three things, they will intertwine to bring joy into my life once again. Amen.

Day 6 - Friday

(Start by lighting the green and blue candles.)

When Becca died, I tried to find other parents to connect with, who could give me hope. But so much of what I found was darkness, despair and hopelessness. I kept hearing that it would never get any better; that I would always be in this horrible place.

I had a hard time with that. I didn't want to stay in this painful and dark place. I wanted to have light in my life, and I wanted to have joy again. I didn't know how, but I knew I would have to fight for it, because I had an enemy that had just robbed me of one of my most prized treasures, and my joy was now buried deep with my daughter.

It is no secret the enemy works overtime to keep us from walking in joy. Why would he be so determined to steal my joy? Because God's joy is my strength.

And I don't mean my joy in Him, I mean His joy in me.

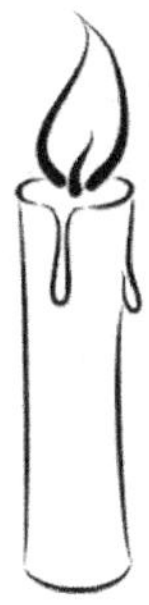

(LIGHT THE YELLOW CANDLE)

Most of us are familiar with Nehemiah 8:10, "...the joy of the Lord is your strength." Do you know how the verse starts? It says, "Do not sorrow, for the joy of the Lord is your strength." And like I said, it is not your joy in Him, but His joy over you.

In the English language (hang in here with me, now) the word "of" is a preposition. If I were to say, "The color of his shirt is ugly," I would not be saying the shirt itself is ugly, but the color is ugly, correct?

If I were to say, "The book of Kevin's is lost," I would not be saying Kevin is lost, I am referring to Kevin's book that is lost, right?

Well, if "the joy of the Lord is my strength", it is referring to the Lord's joy, not mine!

The color of the shirt = the shirt's color

The book of Kevin = Kevin's book.

The joy of the Lord = the Lord's joy

It is the Lord's joy about me that gives me strength, not my joy about Him!

When the Holy Spirit first showed me this, it was a huge relief! I don't have to make sure I have enough joy (based on my love or my happiness in God) to have strength. I don't have to figure out how to manufacture joy in my life to have His strength at work in me.

No, my strength comes from knowing He is crazy in love with me! Wow! Have you ever read Zephaniah 3:17, that tells us how He is rejoicing over us with gladness and singing? It is His joy over me that makes me strong.

It is His joy, His dancing and singing over how much He loves you, that is the strength you can rely on to get you through, *not* your joy over Him. We can take ourselves out of that equation. What a relief, when the thoughts some of us have for Him are not very joyful, or just downright angry.

His joy *about* me creates joy *in* me, which is where my strength comes from to work my way out of the suffocating darkness. Now there is a seed of hope to plant in your life for sure!

Prayer: Father, thank You for the weapon You gave us against the enemy who has stolen our joy. We allow the crazy joy You have for us to make us strong, knowing that Your joy for us will eventually allow our joy to return. Amen.

Day 7 - Saturday

(Start by lighting the green and blue candles.)

How can we possibly smile, or ever be happy again after our child dies? Just the thought of it can make us feel guilty.

But we can, and not only that, it is exactly what we need to do. And we need to reintroduce fun and laughter into our lives, because laughter is medicine to the soul.

If it was reversed (like we all wish it was) would you want your child to remain isolated, depressed and hopeless, believing that life was not worth living without you? Of course not! When we stop and think about it, most of us know in our hearts that our child would not want us to live our lives out that way either.

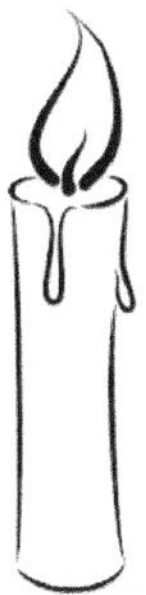

(LIGHT THE YELLOW CANDLE)

"A happy heart is good medicine and a joyful mind causes healing, but a broken spirit dries up the bones," Proverbs 17:22 (AMP).

Joy came that night Jesus was born. We cannot deny that.

When there is a joyful event, there is often dancing. As parents who are in deep grief from the earthly loss of our child, I know we don't feel like dancing, nor do we have the energy, even if we feel a twinge of hope in that direction. At least not on the outside.

But we can dance on the inside. Why would we want to? Because chances are pretty good that is what our child is doing right now, before the throne in heaven. And anything I can do that makes me feel closer to my child, I want to do!

When we are done here, I want you to write your child's name vertically. Then next to each letter, write a word or phrase that starts with that letter as a reason to have joy. What is it about your child that brought joy into your life?

I made myself do it with Becca's name. Here is what I came up with.

Belly laugh

Energy & entertaining (loved to host and decorate and go all out)

Calling and anointing on her life as a worshipper

Compassion and care for others

Adored her family

Once again, here are some powerful words from another pareavor.

> *...She has been gone now for longer than she lived. My life has not stood still; my grief did not hold its shape like concrete. It is a process through which we move, and we return to joy of a different kind, laced with gratitude for what we've had and what we still have... Choose to heal, and you will. Intend it! Then follow the path, step by step, until you're there. (Come Grieve Through Our Eyes)*

It's okay to have hope. It's okay to smile. It's okay to laugh and enjoy life again. From one pareavor to another, I give you permission.

Prayer: Holy Spirit, when we decide to choose life and joy, it is hard work. It is a battle. It can be exhausting. But it can be done through You. Help me to keep going forward, and please keep reminding it that it is so very worth it. Amen.

On this final week, there are only six days of readings in this chapter. You will also notice the days of the week are absent.

This is so that whatever day of the week Christmas falls on, the special Christmas Day reading can be inserted.

Unless Christmas falls on a Saturday, there will still be more readings in this chapter to complete the fourth week.

I highly recommend that you do not just stop on Christmas and put the book away, but return to this chapter, continuing the readings through the end of the week. This will ensure you get the full benefit from this book, *Hope for the Future.*

(Note: If Christmas lands on a Sunday such as 2022, 2033, 2039, 2044 and 2050, you will be one reading short. I suggest using Christmas Eve as your non-reading day, since it is usually just as busy as Christmas, and chances are you will be attending a special church service that evening.

Week Four - LOVE

<u>Day 1</u>

(Start by lighting the green, blue and yellow candles.)

<u>FOREVER</u>

My child,
Flesh of my flesh,
Soul of my soul,
Part of my very being;
I had an instant deep and fierce love when I first saw you.
My heart was yours, and I knew I would give my very life to protect you.

And yet, here I sit, with the suffocating pain and darkness of knowing I was unable to protect you from death.

So now I find that just as deep and intense as my love for you, is the deep and intense pain of my grief in living without you. And yet I know that somehow, I must.

How? How God? How do I go on with a piece of my very being gone from this earth?

And as I ask and seek for this help, God in His tender love, compassion and faithfulness reminds me that I don't have to live without you.

You are forever in my heart and my thoughts, and forever a part of my very being; that our separation is only temporary. You have just moved on to our eternal home before me and have unpacked and settled in, waiting for me and the rest of us to join you.

This isn't a final good-by. It is an "I'll see you later." When I have the thoughts that I would give anything to see you again, to hug you or hear you laugh, I realize that I will! Maybe not as soon as I want to, but it will happen!

And so, I will wait. I will wait with hope, expectancy and even excitement to see you again. Every day I am here on this earth means I am one day closer to that desperate need that I have as a mother to love on you.

And while I wait, I will choose to live my life in a way that is full; full of love, full of peace and contentment, full of laughter. And yet I know it will also still be full of pain and longing. For I have now learned that all of these things can live inside of me together.

So, let me say I am honored. I am honored and blessed to be your mom, and I imagine and dream of our reunion someday, filled with love and joy that goes beyond words to describe it.

But until then, I will have good days and bad days. I will have days filled with happiness, and days filled with pain. And all of those days I will continue to miss you with every fiber of my being.

-By Laura Diehl

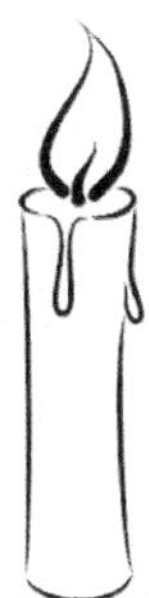

(LIGHT THE RED CANDLE)

"Advent" is a time of waiting. The most common use of the word advent is waiting to celebrate Christmas.

But as pareavors, you and I are much more excited about something else we are waiting for; being reunited with our child.

About a year after Becca died, I confided in a friend that I felt guilty because I was more excited to see Becca in heaven than I was Jesus. She so graciously replied, "But Laura, you've made a deposit there!"

Without the hope of heaven, we could remain in a drowning sea of grief. We will probably never understand why our child had to leave us so soon. That part of child loss will always be a mystery. But with heaven to look forward to, we know we can make it through *today.* And remember, each day we are here is one day closer to being there.

We grieve deeply, because we love deeply. That is one of the risks of love. But as the poem reminds us, our child is forever in our hearts and in our thoughts. He or she is forever a part of our very being. Our separation is only temporary, because God, in His deep love for our child and for us, made a way for that to be possible.

Prayer: Lord, my deep grief is a reminder of my deep love that cannot be poured out on my child right now. But someday we will be together again, and all this stored up love will be dumped on my child! And Father, I ask that right now, you would give my child a big hug from me, and love on them in my place. Thank you. Amen.

Day 2

(Start by lighting the green, blue and yellow candles.)

Christmas is a time of exchanging gifts. You may feel like you don't want any part of that any more.

But let me share with you one gift exchange you will definitely want to be part of. It is the gift exchange of love.

God loves us with an everlasting love. It may not seem like it. We all know He could have, but did not stop the death of our child. That doesn't sound like love to us at all. But wait! Just because we don't understand, just because we don't agree with it, doesn't mean He doesn't love us. It doesn't mean He is a cruel God. What it means is that He can see the full picture that we cannot see.

We think He failed us, but that is impossible. That is part of what makes Him God. It is impossible for Him to fail. Do you know why? Because love never fails, and God *is* love. He doesn't just love as an action; He is love itself.

Do you love your child? Did your child love you? Then that was God. He *is* love. Love is impossible without God being fully involved.

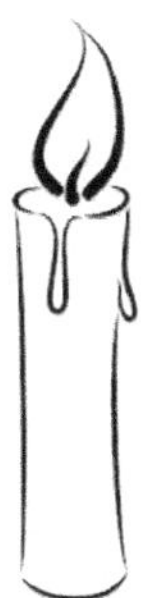

(LIGHT THE RED CANDLE)

An exchange means there is something going both directions. It isn't just God's love being given to us. So, what do we have to give Him back, especially if we are angry at Him?

We give Him the gift of ourselves, anger and all. We tell Him, "Even though You allowed my child to be taken from me on this earth, I have nowhere else to go, nowhere else to turn to heal this shattered heart and pull me out of this place of suffocating darkness. So, I will do my best to receive Your love (that doesn't *feel* like love right now) and I will give myself to You in return; my messed up, full of anger and confused self. I am Yours. Put me back together in all of my brokenness, and break through this wounded heart to feel and know Your love once again."

There is no denying that our wounds go very deep. Having our child die is like an amputation in our very soul and spirit. Our child has been cut off from us, and we need to learn how to live with that piece of us missing.

The effects of your loss will always be there, but God loves you more than you could ever fathom, and He still has a purpose for you.

Our daughter, Becca, had her left leg amputated because of bone cancer when she was only three years old. It was traumatic for all of us. But just like Becca did, in time you can learn how to not only function again, but have an amazing life that can touch others; forever changed by the loss, but also forever changed by the inheritance your child left you.

God so loved, He gave his one and only Son to purchase you, and there are no refunds. He is not taking back His offer, no matter what. The price was paid, you and I are His forever! That is a *good* thing.

Right now, imagine you have a heavy pack on your back. It is full of things like anger, bitterness, resentment, unforgiveness, the heaviness and burden of grief. Take it off your back and lay it down at Jesus' feet; not at the cross, but where He is now, on the throne seated at the right hand of God the Father.

Now in exchange, allow Him to wrap His arms of love around you. It is like a liquid love that just melts into you like a warmth in your very soul. Stay there as long as you want.

Prayer: Father, You paid a high price for us to have this gift exchange. It cost You the life of Your only Son. Help us to remember this gift exchange is always available to us, whenever we need it. Amen.

Day 3

(Start by lighting the green, blue and yellow candles.)

As I have said previously, as a bereaved parent, there are so many scriptures that I have a totally different view of now. A couple of those are part of the Christmas story.

One that makes me shudder is when all those babies age two and under were murdered by order of King Herod as he was trying to snuff out the life of this little baby king that he found out about through the magi looking for him. God warned Joseph in a dream, and they escaped. Why did God allow all of those other families to experience such trauma and horror?

Think of Elizabeth, the mother of John the Baptist. Elizabeth was very old when God finally answered her prayer to have a child. When she gave birth, there was a lot of celebration, because the Lord had shown her great mercy and they shared in her joy. John grew up and prepared the way for Jesus, and during Jesus' ministry, he was beheaded.

Jesus Himself was born for the purpose of dying.

Life and death seem to go together. You cannot have one without the other on this earth.

But God.... God made a way for death not to be a permanent separation from those we love. Why? Because of His great love for each of us.

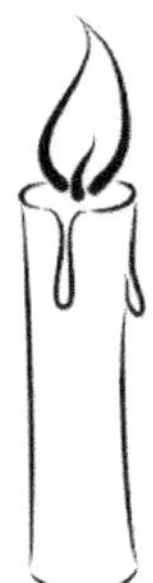

(LIGHT THE RED CANDLE)

Right now, our view of death is limited to our earthly sight. But God has a different view. He shares some of that view with us in Revelation 21:1-6.

> *Then I saw a new heaven and a new earth, for the first heaven and the first earth had passed away, and there was no longer any sea. I saw the Holy City, the new Jerusalem, coming down out of heaven from God, prepared as a bride beautifully dressed for her husband. And I heard a loud voice from the throne saying, "Look! God's dwelling place is now among the people, and he will dwell with them. They will be his people, and God himself will be with them and be their God. 'He will wipe every tear from their eyes. There will be no more death or mourning or crying or pain, for the old order of things has passed away."*
>
> *He who was seated on the throne said, "I am making everything new!" Then he said, "Write this down, for these words are trustworthy and true."*
>
> *He said to me: "It is done. I am the Alpha and the Omega, the Beginning and the End. To the thirsty I will give water without cost from the spring of the water of life,"* (NIV).

John 15:13 tells us that the greatest love we can have is to lay down one's life for one's friends. God laid down His life for *us* through His son, Jesus. That means as our friend, He *knows* what it was like to suffer as a parent who has lost a child.

Why would He *willingly* do that to Himself? Because He loves us! He wants to be in relationship with us. He came down and became part of His creation, including allowing Himself to feel intense pain and sorrow and the darkness of deep grief, so that He could *be* love here on earth to each one of us.

Have you ever been misunderstood? Is there a chance that God is being misunderstood? His deep love for you made Him decide He is willing to take that risk of being misunderstood and rejected in a big way.

Things are not always what they seem. When we give a gift, it must be unwrapped to reveal what is inside. (And sometimes even the box is misleading.) In other words, neither the wrapping on the outside nor the box are the actual gift. It must be fully opened to see what is inside.

I can choose to believe there is no God or He would have saved my child. I can choose to believe that if there is a God, He isn't good and He isn't fair or He would have saved my child. Both of those options leave me feeling angry and empty. I have chosen the third option. There is a God and His thoughts and ways are so much higher than mine, He loves me with a perfect love, and even though I don't understand why He has allowed this to happen, I still trust Him with my life both here on earth and for eternity. This option of unwrapping His gift of love to me, has brought me to a place of peace, rest, hope, and life again–even within the pain.

If I can believe it, and so many other pareavors can believe it, you can too.

Prayer: Lord, I want to believe. Help my unbelief. Help me to look beyond the outside wrappings and see the gift inside; the gift of love You have for me, that will allow me to live in the abundance and the fruit of Your love. Amen.

Day 4

(Start by lighting the green, blue and yellow candles.)

I don't know about you, but I fight against more fears now, since Becca died. The death of our child can bring so many fears into our lives that we never had before. That is very understandable.

However, fear brings torment.

God does not give anyone fear. It comes from the enemy of our souls. As those who have faced the unnatural, out-of-order death of our child, I believe we are huge targets for the enemy's fiery darts of fear that bring torment.

What is the most effective weapon to use against those fears? God's love!

> *There is no fear in love; but perfect love casts out fear, because fear involves torment.* (NKJV) *If we are afraid, it ... shows that we are not fully convinced that He really loves us.* (1 John 4:19 TLB)

That last sentence packs a powerful punch that can hit us right in the gut. Whether we want to admit it or not, we struggle with fear because we are not convinced that God really loves us! If we were convinced He loved us, we would have *faith* in the unknown future instead of fear of the unknown future.

God will throw out the fearful torment of the enemy and replace it with peace, if we run into His arms and trust in His incredible, deep love for us.

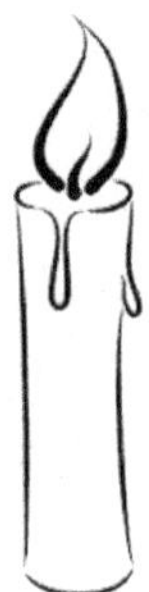

(LIGHT THE RED CANDLE)

During this time of year, *all* of my emotions seem to be magnified. It was much worse those first few years after Becca died. It felt like everything made me sad, which made me cry.

Our tears of grief are the leaking from our hearts of a deep love that has nowhere to go.

And guess what? Jesus Himself had the same leakage! Here is what is recorded in John 11:33-36 (NKJV) when His good friend, Lazarus, died.

> *Therefore, when Jesus saw her weeping, and the Jews who came with her weeping, He groaned in the spirit and was troubled.*
> *And He said, "Where have you laid him?"*
> *They said to Him, "Lord, come and see."*
> *Jesus wept. Then the Jews said, "See how He loved him!"*

Many versions translate the words "groaned in the spirit" to say when Jesus saw everyone crying, he was "deeply moved" and troubled.

There are those who try to explain this as Jesus being troubled by their unbelief that He could raise Lazarus from the dead. But there really is no support for that. In fact, there is more support that Jesus was crying because of grief.

Why do I say that? Because when the story starts, up in verse three we read that the sisters sent for Him with a message saying, "the one You love is sick." That makes me think when Lazarus died, Jesus wept because he was hurting and because He saw how much the family and friends were hurting in their grief.

Why does this even matter? Because you need to know that it is okay to be hurting. It is okay to have groaning and tears in your grief.

And within that, you also need to know that He hurts with you. God isn't telling you that you need to be over it, or that you need to stop being so emotional. People may say those kinds of things to you, but God isn't. (And neither am I.)

In fact, tears are very important to God. He collects them and records them, according to Psalm 56:8. I always say we pareavors must have some of the biggest bottles in heaven, then!

"The hopes and fears of all the years are met in thee tonight." What a wonderful familiar line in one of our common Christmas hymns. We can allow Him to meet all of our needs, whether it is taking away our fears, or being a shoulder for us to cry on. (I like to picture His love like a waterfall; His love just pouring out all over me while the tears run.)

If Jesus wept, so can we.

Prayer: Jesus, thank You for coming into our world and allowing Yourself to feel our hurts and pains, including grief, so that You could relate to us in our brokenness. Sweep us away in Your love that chases our fears and holds our tears. Amen.

<u>Day 5</u>

(Start by lighting the green, blue and yellow candles.)

Emmanuel, God with us. Man has no concept of how much we are loved by God. The only way He could truly convey that love was to actually become one of us and live with us, displaying God's love right in front of us. But even when He was here on earth, He was misunderstood, even to the point of being beaten and murdered.

God's love came in a manger as a baby for the purpose of dying so we could have direct access to that love. He knew He would be misunderstood. He knew He would be falsely accused. But it was worth it. You were worth it.

He is still willing to be misunderstood and falsely accused to give you the choice of love, because it wouldn't be love if it were forced on us and we didn't choose it. And when we stepped into a covenant with God through the blood of Jesus, we stepped into a covenant of His eternal love.

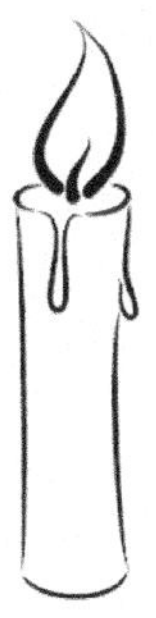

(LIGHT THE RED CANDLE)

Each month, in our ministry Grieving Parents Sharing Hope (GPS Hope), we sell oysters and then open them live while the purchaser watches, to see the beautiful pearl immerge that is theirs to keep.

What does that have to do with anything about our advent journey? Allow me to share part of what gets sent out along with the pearl.

> *The making of a pearl is a miraculous event! Pearls form when an irritant works its way into an oyster. As a defense mechanism, the oyster's body takes defensive action. The oyster begins to secrete a smooth, hard crystalline substance around the irritant in order to protect itself. Layer upon layer of this coating, called 'nacre', is deposited. This process requires a sufficient amount of time - generally at least 3 years - for a thick layer of nacre to be deposited, resulting in a beautiful, gem-quality pearl.*
>
> *Pearls have been highly valued as gemstones and objects of beauty for many centuries. They have a shimmering iridescence, luster and a soft inner glow unlike any other gem on earth. Because of this, a pearl has become a metaphor for something rare, fine, admirable and valuable.*
>
> *YOU are a pearl!*
>
> *You have had something way beyond "an irritant" invade your life. You have had to face the death of your precious child. And now you have the opportunity to allow God to do a far greater miracle in you than He does in an oyster, which is to allow Him the time and tools needed to make something beautiful out of something so horrific.*
>
> *Yes, it can happen. Not only can it happen, but it will happen, if you allow the One who sees what you cannot see, and knows what you do not know to be at work, deeply hidden in your heart and soul, where no one else*

has access. He wants to use this tragedy to make you highly valued; a rare and valuable gem, glowing with His love and glory unlike anyone else on earth.

May this pearl be a symbol of your intense love for your child and the hope of who you can become as a result of that love!

The love God has for you, combined with the love you have for your child, can be a powerful force on this earth!

The person you are becoming is valuable, unique, rare, and precious, and it isn't *in spite* of what has happened, but *because* of it. The love you have for your child can't help but come bursting through at some point, glorious and beautiful, when wrapped in the love of God for both of you.

The word "love" sums up the meaning of Christmas, because the word love sums up the life of Christ.

And because of love, from God and for our child, we can love more deeply than ever and have life with a deeper purpose. That is truly amazing, and something to hope for in our future.

Prayer: God, I thank You that You promise in Your Word (in 1 Peter 5:10) that after I have suffered a while, You will, perfect, establish, strengthen, and settle me. I hold You to that, asking You to make beauty from my ashes that will reflect love; Your love for me, and my love for my child. Amen.

Day 6

(Start by lighting the green, blue and yellow candles.)

Bells have become a symbol of Christmas and we often hear them ringing during the Christmas season. That makes me think of 1 Corinthians 13:1, which tells me that if I do not have love, I am like a noisy gong or a clanging symbol.

After our child dies, we may feel like God's love is like that noisy gong or clanging symbol. But the reality is, His love is more like the bells we hear ringing this time of year. They have a purpose, just like God's love has a purpose. We may have a hard time with that, because we tend to think, "If God really loved me, He wouldn't have let my child die."

But that isn't necessarily love. Love allows choices that affect others. Love does not demand its own way. Love is enduring. Love isn't selfish. And love *never* fails.

I know it may seem impossible to believe, but God did not fail you. It is impossible for Him to fail. He doesn't just love, He *is* love itself, and He is *perfect* love.

Being in a place of such intense darkness in our grief doesn't mean He doesn't love us or that He has failed us. The darkness temporarily blinds us so we can't see the truth. His love for you is just as fierce as it was before you were born and just as fierce as it will be when you join Him in heaven.

During grief, people either move toward God or away from Him. But when we move away from Him, we are moving away from the One who can help us the most. We are pushing away love itself.

God wants to walk with us through this valley of death. He wants to give us comfort. He wants to give us strength. He wants to give us hope. And more than anything, He wants to love on us. These are all things we desperately need. But if we choose to move away from Him and stiff-arm Him, we will continue to desperately need these things.

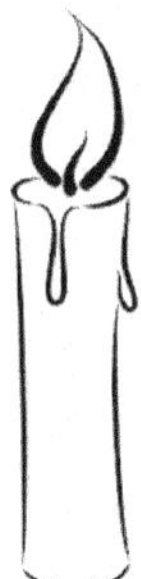

(LIGHT THE RED CANDLE)

Jesus' birth was the beginning of something new. Something that had never been on this earth before... forgiveness and grace... a clean slate.

We need a clean slate.

I am not talking about erasing the memory of our child. I am talking about getting rid of the suffocating pain and darkness.

Bad things happen to good people. Horrible and evil things happen to God's people. You have paid what many will say is the ultimate price of sacrifice on this earth–the death of your son or daughter. (Sound familiar? I know someone else who paid the price of His Son a little over two thousand years ago.) But you did not give your child willingly, or have a choice.

The question is: Are you going to let it be a wasted sacrifice? Are you going to become bitter or better? What value are you going to place on the life of your child?

That is where the clean slate happens. Are you going to choose light and life, or darkness and death?

In Deuteronomy 30:19, God urges us that when life and death are set before us, to "choose life."

> *I refuse to let death cause more death! I will NOT give the enemy that kind of a victory! Because Jesus lives, I can live. I have allowed my God to make good on His promises in my life, to give strength to the weary and hope to the hopeless. And I will allow that hope to continue to grow as it becomes joy that reaches beyond death, both my child's and mine.* (When Tragedy Strikes)

So instead of letting the Christmas season increase your anger at God and push away His incredibly deep love for you, use it as a time to receive the clean slate He came to give. Release yourself from the prison you have found yourself in and get as close to God as you possibly can.

This is the final reading. We will be blowing out the candles of our advent journey for the last time. But don't let the light of hope, peace, joy and love go out in your heart along with the candles. Hold on with everything you have. It is so very worth it.

Let the light of Jesus lead you out of the darkness and believe that there is HOPE for your future.

Prayer: Thank you Father, that the truth sets us free. May the truth of Your love set us free, giving us a clean slate to live in the abundance of hope, peace, and joy. Amen.

Christmas Day

(Start by lighting the green, blue, yellow and red candles.)

Our life here on earth is not a destination. It is a journey.

When we are going on a trip, sometimes we make plans, knowing exactly where we are going, and get there without any problems. Sometimes we know where we want to go, but need a map or GPS to guide us to the right place. And sometimes the road changes and even the GPS has no idea where we are!

That is how we feel after the death of our child. We feel lost and helpless, not knowing where we are going, much less how to get there.

Jesus was born into a world of darkness, unbelief and confusion. He was born as the Light of the World. Even death could not put out that light, because not only was He born to die, but also to be resurrected. He came to bring light into the deepest darkness. He came to bring resurrection life from death.

Not just death that causes our bodies to quit and our spirits to leave them, but the death that happens in our souls after the death of our child.

That is where "Emmanuel, God with us" comes in. He becomes our guide in the darkness. He knows where the path is, and will help us navigate to each road we need to be on while traveling this grief journey.

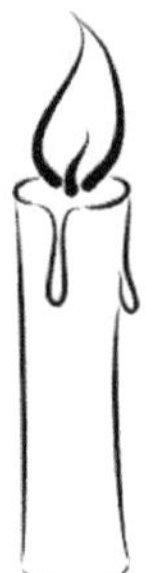

(LIGHT THE WHITE CANDLE)

If you were to see pictures of baby Jesus in other cultures, you might be surprised. To the Africans, Jesus is a little black baby. To the Chinese, He has slanted eyes and yellow skin. To the Germans, He has big blue eyes and yellow curls. To the Mexicans, He has olive skin, brown eyes and dark hair. What is so awesome about this is that He is so real, so personal, that He belongs to each of us. He really is Emmanuel, God with us.

Eternity doesn't just start for us when we die. It starts as soon as we are born. Eternal, resurrection life is available to us all now, in this life here on earth. Jesus came to bring God's resurrection power into our lives *while* we are here on this earth, not just after we die and leave this earth.

Each of us has a set number of days here on this old earth, and then we move on to the glorious side of eternity. Our child's time here was much too short as far as we are concerned, and we were supposed to go first.

But the fact remains, our child has now moved on to his or her permanent home, and is more alive and full of life than we are! For reasons we don't understand, God decided their purpose on earth was completed before ours was.

So now it is important that we continue moving forward in *our* earthly purpose, so that when we join our child who is waiting for us, we will hear the wonderful words, "Well done, good and faithful servant...Enter into the joy of your Lord" (Matthew 25:21 NKJV).

Yes, there *is* hope in your future. But not just your future in eternity after you die, but in eternity now, while living out your time here on earth.

There is hope in your future because He *is* Emmanuel, God with us. Not only is He the coming King who will be riding on a white horse in the clouds, but He is here with us now, dwelling inside of our very being, comforting us, guiding us, and bringing light back into our darkness.

Prayer: Jesus, on Christmas Day, I celebrate Your light that pierced the deepest darkness when you came to earth. You are truly Emmanuel, God with us. And because Jesus came as a baby, lived here on earth, died and rose again, I know that death is not the end for my child or myself. Thank you for the hope I have in my future, not just when I leave this earth, but while I am still here, as I navigate my purpose without my child here with me. Amen.

Would you like a chance to go deeper?

Grieving the death of our child can be a lonely place.

Those who have not experienced that suffocating darkness may have good intentions, but can rarely offer the help and hope we need, as they cannot relate to the depth of our unique loss.

It can also be hard to connect with those who *do* understand, for various reasons. If it is going to a meeting or a conference, we might not have the finances, the time, or the energy.

And then we can find that we are often torn between wanting to be with others who get it, and *not* wanting to be with others who get it. Maybe we just don't want to be around a group of people, no matter who they are, or we are afraid that being with others who are a "mess like me" will make me feel even worse.

I get it. That is why we are doing our best to create opportunities to have someone who is ahead of you on this journey walk with you in the privacy of your own home.

- First, we have made available an online conference, called "The Hope and Healing Virtual Summit." Depending on when you check, you may be able to get in on it for free when we first post the newest summit. If not, we always make each year available in our store.

  To find out if we have a live one coming up, who the speakers are each year, get more details, or find out how to purchase the past online conferences to watch at your own pace, in privacy on your own digital device, go to www.gpshope.org/virtualsummit. (This webpage will also allow you to **download a free session** from the 2017 virtual summit.)

- Second, we have a course that can be taken based on Laura's award-winning book *When Tragedy Strikes: Rebuilding Your Life with Hope and Healing after the Death of Your Child.*

  This course has three levels, based on how little or how much input you want on your journey.

  > Level one: A mini-course that walks you through some of the most difficult parts of a pareavor's journey
  >
  > Level two: A full course, taking a deeper dive based on all twelve chapters of *When Tragedy Strikes*
  >
  > Level three: The full course, along with personal coaching from Laura

  To find out more, go to www.gpshope.org/wtscourse.

We hope you will take a look at both of these opportunities and connect to the one you believe will be the most help to you, as we continue this journey together.

About the Author

Laura Diehl is passionate about extending a light of hope to bereaved parents. Through her writing, speaking and coaching, she walks with grieving parents in their place of darkness, without judgement or shame, to learn how to live a life of meaning and purpose once again.

Laura found herself in a place of suffocating darkness after the death of her daughter, Becca, with no one to turn to for help in navigating out of the deep pit of grief. Today, as a bereaved mom living a life of fulfillment, purpose and destiny, Laura invests her time in helping grieving parents journey from a place of brokenness, to becoming a repurposed vessel in a way that honors the life of their child, instead of living in the shadow of their child's death.

She is the cofounder, along with her husband, of Grieving Parents Sharing Hope (GPS Hope) which serves the "club" no one wants to be in, and has no way out - the unique and precious community of bereaved parents. Laura and her husband, Dave, live in Southern Wisconsin, and have five children (one in heaven and four here on earth) and a growing legacy of grandchildren.

Other books by Laura Diehl

When Tragedy Strikes: Rebuilding Your Life With Hope and Healing After the Death of Your Child

As a grieving parent, there can be a feeling of desperation to find someone farther ahead on the path who can understand the crushing pain that makes you feel like you can't even breathe at times. Laura Diehl was plunged into that place of darkness with the death of her daughter, and meets the deep need to connect with others who have experienced what cannot be put into words. The award winning book, *When Tragedy Strikes,* is the raw account of her journey from deep darkness back into light and life, extending a hand of hope to those traveling on the path behind her, who need to rebuild their lives after the death of a child.

Endorsed by

- Wayne Jacobson, coauthor of *The Shack*
- Darrell Scott, founder of Rachel's Challenge, author, father of Rachel Scott killed in Columbine school shooting (age seventeen)
- Dr. Gloria Horsley, International Grief Counselor, founder of Open to Hope, mother of Scott (age seventeen)
- Several ministry leaders and pastors
- Many bereaved parents

Come Grieve Through Our Eyes: How to Give Comfort And Support To Bereaved Parents By Taking A Glimpse Into Our World Of Grief

Come Grieve Through Our Eyes gives a clear, truthful message from those who have lost a child, to those who want to know how to be there for these grieving parents. This book opens the door into the world of bereaved parents, enabling the readers to go beyond just condolences and sympathy, but having compassion at a level that will help these devastated parents at their deepest level of need.

Many pareavors have also found this book very helpful, as it lets them know they are not alone or unusual in their struggles.

My Grief Journey: Coloring Book and Journal for Grieving Parents

Are you a grieving parent, looking for ways to help relieve the intense pain, anger, and confusion? Do you want to move toward hope and life again?

Search the internet, and you will find all kinds of studies to prove that coloring relieves stress. Journaling also helps us get in touch with things we might be feeling, but haven't been able to put into words. This book, *My Grief Journey: Coloring Book and Journal* puts the two together.

Each page has a word (for example, confusion, helpless, anger, future, hope, comfort, thankful, etc.) surrounded by beautiful artwork. Also on the page, you will find a scroll, with a prompt for writing your thoughts and emotions about that word. On the page next to it, you will find where author, Laura Diehl, shares her own thoughts about that word, along with a verse from the Bible.

For those who purchase *My Grief Journey: Coloring Book and Journal for Grieving Parents* there is a private Facebook page, where photos of the colored pages can be shared, and those grieving can be a community of hope and encouragement for one another. To be part of this group, go to www.facebook.com/groups/mygriefjourney

My Grief Journey: Coloring Book and Journal for Kids

Do you know a child who has faced a deep loss, such as the death of a parent, sibling or grandparent? Are you looking for a way to help them sort out their thoughts and emotions? *My Grief Journey: Coloring Book and Journal for Kids* is for any age (including adult "kids") who are learning how to live after the death of someone dearly loved and deeply missed.

- Each coloring page has a word surrounded by beautiful artwork which is intentionally hand drawn.
- Each word has two pages to help the child think about and explore a specific word or emotion (such as helpless, fear, memories, hope, comfort, truth, thankful, etc.) through coloring, drawing and writing.
- The coloring page has a scroll with a "prompt," to help them get started in thinking how they might feel about something.

- The prompt can be answered inside the scroll by either writing or drawing.
- We have also included an extra page for each word to allow more room for drawing or writing.

This book is a simplified version of *My Grief Journey: Coloring Book and Journal for Grieving Parents*, using twenty-nine of the forty-two words (and adding one word not in the adult book). This was done intentionally, so that a parent and child can do many of the pages together, if there has been a sibling loss for the child.

From Ring Bearer to Pallbearer: Giving a Voice to Bereaved Siblings and Grandparents

Well-meaning people fail to recognize the depth of the loss of someone who has lost a sibling, making them feel their intense pain isn't valid, and they are not supposed to be hurting so deeply. Grandparents are another group whose grief can get lost in the death of a child. They not only lose their legacy and the relationship with their grandchild, but have to watch their own adult child go through the horrible suffering and trauma at the death of their child. *From Ring Bearer to Pallbearer* shares the thoughts of Laura's youngest son who was a ring bearer for his sister's wedding at age six, and a pallbearer for her casket at age 16. The other two brothers share as well, along with all four grandparents. You will see just how different each one is, but they are all valid, just like the grief of every sibling and grandparent is valid.

This book is exclusive to GPS Hope and not available in bookstores. WE WOULD LIKE TO GIVE YOU A FREE DIGITAL COPY. Just go to www.gpshope.org/free-library, click on the link to register as a new member and fill in your name, email, and a password.

Triple Crown Transformation: Finding Your Rightful Royal Place in God's Kingdom

Attaining the Triple Crown is a rare accomplishment, whether in horse racing or in baseball. Unfortunately, it is also a rare accomplishment in our lives as a Christian. What is the Triple Crown for a Christian? Laura Diehl believes it is learning:

1. How to clarify God's vision for our lives, including being released from our past which keeps us from going forward
2. how to live from a place of authority of being in Christ
3. how to live from a deeper revelation of the identity of the indwelling power of the Holy Spirit.

She has dealt with all of these issues through some pretty dark trials, including what many say is the worst thing a person can ever face in this life. Find out what she has learned about vision, authority, and identity in God's Kingdom. See the Crown...Wear the Crown...Be the Crown!

(Laura's books can be found for sale on www.gpshope.org **or your favorite bookstore.)**

Visit Us Online

www.gpshope.org

Grieving Parents Sharing Hope (GPS Hope) is a place for those who are going through the deep dark blackness of losing a child, to find encouragement and strength. It is a safe place for the shattered hearts of pareavors (bereaved parents) to take off their masks and be allowed to grieve as needed.

Dave and Laura Diehl's faith in God and belief in His ability to give them a life again beyond the death of their daughter, pulled them out of that deep black pit that pareavors know all too well. That same faith in God has led them to where they are now, and where they continue to walk, one day at a time. They have learned to persevere and push past the tragic event, going beyond hope, to a place with fullness of purpose and meaning.

GPS Hope was birthed because Dave and Laura Diehl believe this is possible for *all* pareavors. It exists to give direction to hope, healing, and light, by offering various tools and resources to this unique group of parents.

At the GPS Hope website, you will find:

- A free members library with lots of downloadable tools and resources
- A Wall of Remembrance where a parent can have a picture of their child posted along with a paragraph about their child
- The Expressions of Hope blog

- The GPS Hope store
- A link to our events page

As mentioned on Day 5 in the fourth week of this book, we have a **monthly Pearls of Hope event.** One hundred percent of the proceeds of this FUNdraiser, benefits GPS Hope, to be able to reach more pareavors in their place of darkness. For more information or to find out how to order an oyster, go to www.gpshope.org/pearls.

GPS Hope also has a **Facebook page**, which can be found at www.facebook.com/gpshope.

www.gpshope.org

Looking for a powerful speaker for an event?

Consider bringing Laura in to share with your group how to have a firm grip on their faith in God when the storms of life blow, and to impart hope into those who may be losing that grip.

> *Since my passion is helping orphans, there isn't much that moves me outside of that. But when Laura speaks I am always deeply touched, which is why I give her one of my top speaking spots at my conferences.* - Tom Stamman, founder of Impact Ministries, International.

> *Laura has joined me in the U.S. and internationally in women's conferences and other ministries to teach, speak and preach the Word Of God. She has used her gifts and talents to uplift, inspire, cheer and bring hope to all that she comes in contact with. This action-oriented servant has been most successful in using her gifts and talents by bringing together a fragmented world in perfect harmony as God wills.* - J.P. Olson, Founder of Journey Into The Word Ministry and Today's Women Empowerment Summit.

Laura also loves to share and minister directly to bereaved parents.

To submit a request form, go to www.lauradiehlauthor.com.

Laura Diehl, Grief Journey Coach

Have you ever wished you had another bereaved parent who was further along in their grief journey to personally help you navigate through the swirling waters of grief?

Have you ever thought about connecting directly to a pareavor who will personally help you get back to a place of hope, light and a fulfilled life with purpose and meaning once again?

If so, you might want to consider looking at Laura Diehl's coaching programs which are only made available two or three times a year.

To find out if she has any openings, contact Laura at laura@gpshope.org.

Made in the USA
Middletown, DE
23 November 2020

24958468R00080